"I have seen in your eyes a fire of determination to get this war job done quickly. My confidence in you is total, our cause is just. Now you must be the thunder and lightning of Desert Storm."

—Gen. H. Norman Schwarzkopf
16 JANUARY 1991
RIYADH, SAUDI ARABIA

AN INSIDER'S VIEW OF THE COMMANDER AND HIS VICTORY

★ ★

Schwarzkopf

LT. COL. ROBERT D. PARRISH, USA, RET.
and COL. N.A. ANDREACCHIO, USA, RET.

BANTAM BOOKS
NEW YORK • TORONTO • LONDON • SYDNEY • AUCKLAND

SCHWARZKOPF
A Bantam Nonfiction Book / May 1991

ISBN 0-553-29573-x

Published simultaneously in the United States and Canada

PRINTED IN THE UNITED STATES OF AMERICA

RAD   0 9 8 7 6 5 4 3 2 1

*To the men and women
who were killed
in the Persian Gulf War,
and to their families.*

Acknowledgments and Comment

The authors are indebted to many people and organizations who graciously provided information for this book. Particularly valuable were the insights provided by officers who served with General Schwarzkopf from his days as a West Point cadet to this command of CENTCOM.

Many agencies, including the Department of Defense, the Department of the Army, the United States Central Command, and various corps and division headquarters were quite supportive. (Their quick responses and detailed information were in part prompted by the authors' knowing the right people to contact.)

We would particularly like to thank all our former Army, Navy, and Air Force colleagues, from sergeant to general, who came through when they were needed. We owe you one.

Finally, we'd like to thank Lt. Col. (USA, Ret.) Jim MacDonald, who prepared the appendices.

At the time of Desert Shield and Desert Storm our own experience and professional training were very useful in seeing past the press briefings and often inaccurate news reports. They were even more important in writing this book.

In the next years, there will be many more stories told and much more detail released about the Persian Gulf War. Then the true magnitude of

what General H. Norman Schwarzkopf and his
people accomplished will be even more impressive.
Norm Schwarzkopf's real contribution was that he
knew nothing was impossible, so convinced his
people to do it.

CONTENTS

★ ★ **I** ★ ★

THE MAKING OF A GENERAL

★ ★ **II** ★ ★

DESERT SHIELD

★ ★ III ★ ★

DESERT STORM

★ ★ IV ★ ★

AFTERWARD

MAPS AND DIAGRAMS

I

THE
MAKING
OF
A GENERAL

THE MAN AND HIS
ARMY

He commands the largest U.S. fighting force since Vietnam. His sleeping area is a small room next to his office. He loathes commanders who live in luxury while the troops are in the field. He says he is antiwar. He has been wounded in action, received three Silver Stars, three Bronze Stars, and the Distinguished Service Medal. He is a paratrooper, yet he has committed to combat one of the largest armored and mechanized forces in United States history. He has an IQ of 170 and is a member of the International Brotherhood of Magicians. He has a terrible temper, but outstanding officers fight to serve under him.

He is six feet, three inches, and 240 pounds of fierce and intimidating determination, yet his deep concern for the welfare of the individual soldier is genuine and well known. He has picked up various nicknames along the way, some of which bring to mind overwhelming force: "Stormin' Norman," "The Bear," and "Arc Light," a reference to a massive B-52 bomb strike. Yet these seeming contradictions are only part of the whole man—the man who achieved for his country one of the most lopsided victories in history, a victory that was achieved with stunningly few casualties to his soldiers.

Some of the envious will say he was lucky and just happened to be in the right place at the right time. Others will disagree, saying that he made his own luck. But all will agree that he was in the right place at the right time for the United States of America.

How did he just "happen" to be there when his country needed him? If one takes only a cursory look at his life, one might only see a successful, but generally "normal" career. But if one looks a little deeper, it becomes clear that the path of newly commissioned Second Lieutenant "Schwarzie" Schwarzkopf of 1956 was already set for the position of Commander-in-Chief (CINC) of the United States Central Command of 1991. The man made the career, and the career made him CINC.

Trying to understand General H. Norman Schwarzkopf without understanding the Army in which he grew and served would be like asking a man who had never seen water to describe the development of a fish. The Army is its own world, its own way of life, with strong standards and many unwritten rules that are as firmly established as any written law. Despite the impressions that some civilians have of it, the Army is never static. It is constantly changing and reforming itself and its soldiers. In some areas changes seem to come slowly, but in others the pace is fast and furious. The Army that Second Lieutenant Schwarzkopf entered in 1956, that Lieutenant Colonel Schwarzkopf fought with in Vietnam in 1969, and that General Schwarzkopf commanded in the Persian Gulf in 1991 are all vastly different institutions. It's easy to see the differences in the uniforms, weapons, equipment, and technology. It's much harder to see the changes in its feelings and attitudes—its soul—but that, too, has changed dramatically. But some things haven't changed: the need for good soldiers, sound leadership, and an officer corps that follows the creed of "Duty, Honor, and Country."

★

As is often the case with young men, when Norman started on his path to Saudi Arabia he was following in his father's footsteps. Proving that truth is stranger than fiction, Norm was in Iran when he was only twelve years old, giving new meaning to the expression "long range reconnaissance." He wasn't actually looking for future avenues of attack, just responding to his father's invitation to join him in Iran for a year. The senior Schwarzkopf's career, even in outline, reads like an adventure story. Commissioned at West Point in 1917, he left the Army after the war to take charge of the New Jersey State Police. He investigated the Lindbergh kidnapping case and even narrated "Gang Busters," a popular radio show of the time. Ordered back to active duty after Pearl Harbor, he was sent to Iran to organize and train Iran's National Police Force, so it would be able to protect the U.S. supply routes that ran through Iran to the Soviet Union. Schwarzkopf senior was there when the war ended, and he sent for his twelve-year-old son to join him. It isn't difficult to imagine what an adventure this was for a twelve-year-old who was young enough to dream of excitement, yet old enough to appreciate and remember when the dream came true. Following the father was natural, but it was also fortunate because the senior Schwarzkopf provided his son with a set of moral and ethical standards that served the boy and then the man well.

These standards were strongly reinforced at the United States Military Academy at West

Point. In 1951, the year before young Norm entered the Academy, West Point expelled several cadets who had violated its rigid honor code: "I will not lie, cheat, or steal; and I will not tolerate those who do." It was the first big honor code violation in modern times, so when Schwarzkopf arrived at the Academy the honor code was receiving even greater emphasis than before. This served to drive home what Norm had learned from his father. Thirty-five years later, one of his former subordinates would remark that (then) Colonel Schwarzkopf taught him that being honest and doing right *does* work, and that one doesn't have to compromise his principles to be successful.

West Point is very structured and demanding, and competition is not only encouraged, but forced. For example, the cadet—and everyone else—is constantly told of his standing in the class. Class standing not only determines who stays and who goes, it also determines the branch (infantry, artillery, engineer, and so forth) you will be assigned to upon graduation. There are only a limited number of openings in each branch, and the top cadets are given their choice. The unfortunate young man (and now possibly young woman) who graduates at the bottom of the class gets whatever branch vacancy is left.

Norman, or "Schwarzie" as he was called in

those days, did very well, especially in mechanical engineering. When graduation time rolled around he was in the top ten percent of his class. It was then that he made a major decision that would affect his career and the rest of his life. It would see him honored for his battlefield exploits, cause him to pay for those honors with his own blood, and make him a national hero. Cadet H. Norman Schwarzkopf chose infantry.

Within the Army, each branch is a soldier's fraternity, and like a frat it has its own traditions, insignia, color, standards, and measures of success. But it is more than a club; it's a family within a family. Throughout an officer's entire military career he will serve with the same group of people. Most of his best friends will be in the same branch. The husbands of his wife's friends will be mostly of that branch. The wives will raise their kids together, often while their husbands are gone for months or years at a time. The families will help each other, not just with routine things, but in real crises. Should the dreaded knock at the door come, a soldier's fellow branch officers and their wives will do much more than just cry at his funeral.

An officer earns his reputation first within his branch; once earned it follows or precedes him for the rest of his career. With dedication and hard work he can build a good reputation. With less dedication, even if only momentary, he can destroy his reputation.

Similar branches are grouped according to their mission. For example, infantry, armor, and artillery are collectively known as the "combat arms." Engineer, signal, and similar branches are called "combat support." Quartermaster, transportation, and others are "combat service support." In each case the operative word is "combat," because that's what the Army is all about. Everyone either fights or supports those who do.

Beyond the branch, soldiers identify with their groups, and make jokes about others who do not have similar missions. Tankers will rib infantrymen, and the "grunts" as they proudly call themselves, will respond with equal, but good-natured sarcasm. There is a brotherhood among similar branches, but much less so between groups. Combat arms soldiers often make biting remarks about combat support and combat service support. Support troops usually respond with unfavorable characterizations of the combat soldiers' intelligence. It's only when they face a common enemy or the civilian world outside that they refer to themselves simply as "soldiers."

Certainly the decision by a "ten percenter" to choose Infantry as his branch was not unusual. Many have done so in the past and will in the future, but it does speak well for a young man to select the toughest branch of service when he has other attractive options. There are many jokes about the different branches, but there is one thing everyone agrees on—the infantry is the toughest, most uncomfortable, most dangerous and, some would say, the most unappreciated branch in the Army. In combat there is no comparison with the other branches. Even the tanker gets to ride while the grunt "humps" a hundred-pound pack. On the battlefield the infantry is often alone in a world that has gone totally mad, expected to close with and destroy the enemy. The infantryman actually encounters individual enemy soldiers, sometimes coming as close as the bayonet on the end of his rifle.

Norm Schwarzkopf chose to be an infantry-man. When he did, he added the infantry's motto to his personal honor code—"Follow me!"

2

★ ★ ★ ★

LIEUTENANT
SCHWARZKOPF

S econd Lieutenant Schwarzkopf's first assignment was to the 2d Airborne Battle Group, 187th Infantry, of the 101st Airborne Division, the "Screaming Eagles" of Bastogne fame. At that unit's peacetime headquarters at Fort Campbell, Kentucky, he was introduced to the "glamorous" and exciting life of a young officer in the post-Korea Army. Besides the full-time mission of training his men and looking out for their welfare, he got all the unwanted jobs that every young officer receives. Second Lieutenant Schwarzkopf, the very lowest ranking officer on the base, had to catch all the "stuff" that naturally runs down hill. There were inventories of the stock in the commissary, officers' and enlisted clubs, and post exchanges. There were inspections of the mess halls. There were twelve- and twenty-four-hour stints as officer of the guard and officer of the day.

There was also duty as counsel on court-martials. In those days, before the explosion of trained lawyers, unit officers handled lower-level trials. Lieutenants usually acted as defense counsel or prosecutor (trial counsel). Captains, majors, and sometimes lieutenant colonels formed the jury, with the senior officer acting as judge. If a soldier was found guilty of a serious offense, he could be sentenced to imprisonment for six months or more.

Then there were investigations of missing or damaged property, which could lead to a fellow officer's career being ended. This was particularly hard, as the investigation was invariably supervised by the sourest captain in the battalion, whose philosophy of property accountability was simply, "If you have too many, you must have stolen it; if you don't have enough, you must have sold it." Knowing the possible consequences for an individual responsible for missing or misappropriated property was a real test of the honor code.

All these tasks were called "additional duties," because that is what they were—additions to Lieutenant Schwarzkopf's demanding job as a platoon leader. Even in peacetime it was his awesome responsibility to ensure that his men were well trained, properly equipped, healthy, and well fed, and that their morale was high. This was the world that Lieutenant Schwarzkopf and other second lieutenants entered. It is also one aspect of the Army that hasn't changed to this day.

On the surface it seems like a terrible experience to put young officers through, but underneath there is a logic to it all. First, these things have to be done by someone, and that has to be as an additional duty. As a defense or trial counsel Lieutenant Schwarzkopf learned the military justice system, and that experience would greatly benefit both himself and his soldiers later in his career. He learned how to manage supplies and take care of government property. He learned how important food, recreation, and time off are to a soldier. He learned to handle and help solve the many personal problems his men had. While doing his many jobs, Norm learned that he genuinely liked the American soldier, and that these "extra" assignments were the really fun part of the Army.

But the two most important lessons he learned were how to juggle more than two balls at once, and that the Army held him *personally* responsible for everything his unit did, or failed to do. Being merely a second lieutenant was not an acceptable excuse for failure. A young officer either learned those lessons or left the Army. Lieutenant Schwarzkopf didn't leave.

The Army was smaller in those days and money was tight. The soldiers hadn't received a pay raise in several years. There weren't sufficient funds for the training the Army wanted and needed to do, but everything was still very competitive and driven by numbers. Inspections received scores. Units like infantry rifle platoons, artillery batteries, and tank battalions were tested in field exercises and given a numerical grade. Success or failure, promotion or pass over all depended upon a set of numbers. The Army lived then as it does now, on competition. It is a philosophy based on the fact that second place in war means you and the nation have lost.

The 101st Airborne Division was considered an elite unit with tough readiness requirements to match its mission to be ready to move quickly anywhere in the world to fight an enemy. It was a very tough "school" for the beginner, and only the most capable survived. In jump school, where Lieutenant Schwarzkopf earned his silver paratrooper's wings, and later at the 101st Airborne, he became caught up in what has been called the "airborne mystic." Simply stated, it means that airborne soldiers believe they are the best. They know that one airborne soldier can beat at least ten of the enemy on the battlefield, and at least twice that number of non-airborne "leg" soldiers in a bar fight. This is the kind of esprit-de-corps that all units strive to instill in their men, and to its credit no one has been more successful at it than the Airborne.

Norm's introduction to the real Army was tough and demanding, and he was given almost no slack. He served as platoon leader and later as executive officer of Company E. He got his first taste of staff duty when he was assigned as the assistant operations officer, a prize assignment for a young officer who had served as a platoon leader. Norm Schwarzkopf soldiered well and not only survived, but was more successful than many of his contemporaries. If he hadn't known what his capabilities were before joining the 101st Airborne, he knew now—and so did a lot of other people.

His next assignment was to the Berlin Brigade, where he would have his first taste of larger unit operations. It was a small, but definite step on the way to high command. He was no longer a second lieutenant and could at last avoid some of the more strenuous additional duties. Berlin, always viewed as one of the Army's better assignments, with a good social life and an opportunity to travel throughout Europe, offered great training opportunities backed by the money to do it. The Berlin Brigade was more independent than many other units, and more generously funded through agreement with the West German government—so much so that it was often said that there were two armies, the one in the United States and the one in Europe. The army in Europe received the lion's share of training opportunities. With a strong dollar and the threat from the Soviet Union, the emphasis was on Europe. It was one of the few places in the world where a commander could leave his post with his tanks and armored personnel carriers and conduct maneuvers practically anywhere he wished. That couldn't be done in the United States, where any commander who even considered it would be committed for psychiatric observation. The army in Europe was—and still is—the United States's maneuvers army. It certainly helped Desert Storm to have a commander-in-chief who knew that army and could draw two highly trained armored divisions from it.

Each unit in Germany had its own local training area, as well as access to major training areas elsewhere in the country. Grafenwohr was the largest major training area, and units like the Berlin Brigade rotated there for weeks at a time. Until the development of The National Center in the southern California desert, nothing even remotely comparable existed in the United States.

Units stationed in Europe spent as much as fifty percent of their time away from their home station. That (and being in a foreign country) brought the officers and men close and they got to know each other very well. "Male bonding" wasn't a popular phrase in those days, but the process was very real. At the same time, the wives were left alone with the children and learned to rely on each other. Many of the customs looked upon with a degree of scorn today, such as coffees and teas, were the wives' only escape from a very demanding and lonely life. The motto "The Army takes care of its own" was very true, but it was the people and not the institution who took care of each other.

Despite the low pay and the lack of funds (compared to today), those days in Germany were really a Golden Age for training in the Army. Standards were high, with unannounced alerts called at all hours of the night. The alerts were not just called, the units were checked. If a unit failed to get on the road to its designated combat position, or was found lacking in any aspect of readiness to fight, a commander's career could end abruptly. The vehicles had to run, the soldiers had to be ready with their equipment and weapons, and the unit had to be ready to go. Lieutenant Schwarzkopf was responsible for this in his unit.

Leaves and even overnight passes for the officers and men were restricted to a certain percentage of the unit's strength. The individual soldier seldom received a long pass to go into town, and bed check was conducted every night.

Discipline was strict and harsh for all, not just the private. A sergeant who failed to do well at the noncommissioned officer academy could kiss at least one stripe goodbye. And a poor showing during an alert, inspection, or training test could be fatal to an officer's career.

This was the Army that Norman joined after he left the 101st Airborne Division, one of the most combat-ready and well-trained units in the United States Army. No one could have received a better grounding in what the Army was supposed to be than an officer who had consecutive assignments in the elite 101st Division and then Germany. To succeed in either, that officer had to be able to establish priorities and then remain focused on them despite the many distractions that invariably occurred. The vast majority of Army officers do well in establishing priorities, but the ability to maintain that focus and push the right priorities is much rarer. "Focus," "determination," and "persistence" are the words most often heard in descriptions of H. Norman Schwarzkopf's move up the ranks. Another word, "intimidation," was added later, but not always in a pejorative manner. Even a Santa Claus standing six feet, three inches tall and weighing 240 pounds would be intimidating. But no one has ever heard Norm being likened to Santa Claus.

In Berlin he got his first view of operations at

a high level when he was selected to serve as aide-de-camp to the Commanding General of Berlin Command. The selection of an aide-de-camp depends mainly on the personality of the general for whom he will work. Theoretically, a young officer with promise is chosen, with the idea of exposing him to the big picture and, hopefully, preparing him for bigger things in the future. But the potential in the position is very dependent on the general officer: He can help the officer develop or just use him as an errand boy. Nothing is automatic in the aide-de-camp business and it is not always, to use an Army buzz word, "career enhancing." The job also depends on how the aide interacts with his general's subordinates and superiors. A successful aide does *not* follow the words of Francis Grose in his advice to the British Army in 1782: "Let your deportment be haughty and insolent to your inferiors, humble and fawning to your superiors, solemn and distant to your equals."

An aide's job is a most challenging balancing act, and one that is not always handled well by a young officer. One day the officer is one of the boys, but the next he is one of "them." Soaring with the eagles can be exhilarating, but mighty dangerous if the officer doesn't recognize he is not an eagle. The most common pitfall is an aide's assuming some of the mantle of the commander. His is, or can be, a powerful position, and people much senior to him may seek his advice on how the old man is feeling today, or "How do you think the general feels about this idea?" With the best of intentions, the aide can subtly push an idea that *he thinks* the general likes and thereby get himself into real trouble. The corruption of power can affect lieutenants and captains as well as princes and kings.

Equally dangerous is the aide's relationship with his friends. Should Lieutenant Schwarzkopf drop a hint to a good friend that the general is going to hit his unit with a surprise inspection, one that could affect the friend's career? How Lieutenant Schwarzkopf handled these personal and professional situations could not help but affect his entire career. Memories are long, and any abuse of his position would have come back to haunt him. As the old saying goes, "What goes around, comes around." Yet, with all these dangers, there was also an unparalleled opportunity for the young officer to gain insight into how the Army really works at the top levels. That Berlin was an international community was a bonus— Norm was exposed to some of the problems that arise when dealing with allies. In that sense Berlin has always had the aura of a combination political-military assignment. That exposure early in his career prepared Lieutenant Schwarzkopf for both Vietnam and Saudi Arabia.

In September 1961, the Army's professional

development program came into play, and Norm was selected to attend the Infantry Officers Advance Course at Fort Benning, Georgia. He was now a captain and had been at the unit level for almost five years, with time to prepare for higher command and staff positions.

The Army probably has the most structured professional education system of any of the services, and it is selective, not voluntary. Periodically throughout their careers, successful officers are picked to attend service schools as an integral part of their professional development. The selection for each level of school is more competitive than the last. Failure to be chosen for the next higher level sends a clear signal: The officer's career has slowed, has stopped, or is about to end. Selection for schooling is second only to being selected for promotion, and it normally tells the officer that he will be promoted. Thus, officers and their wives anxiously await the publication of the list of attendees for each course. Because the school lists are also published in the *Army Times* newspaper, everyone knows who did or did not get selected.

While there have been changes in emphasis through the years, the professional system has remained essentially the same. A "basic course," exactly what the name implies, is what a newly commissioned second lieutenant must attend before he goes to his first assignment. A few years later the officer becomes eligible for the branch advanced course, oriented toward preparing senior first lieutenants and captains for staff assignments at brigade and division level. During Schwarzkopf's time, it also prepared them for the command of a company, if they hadn't already been in command. In those days the Army sent all the officers it expected to retain on active duty (or in the reserves) to both the basic and advanced courses. After that, the chances of an officer's being selected for a higher level of schooling dropped dramatically.

The ax falls hard when a board of senior army officers chooses the majors and new lieutenant colonels who will get to attend the Command and General Staff College at Fort Leavenworth, Kansas. Only about thirty-five percent of all eligible officers are picked for this course, and it's from that small group that future generals will be chosen. It is an academic year long and teaches officers how divisions, corps, and armies operate both in peacetime and in war. It tells them what they need to know to work on the staffs of the Department of the Army, Department of Defense, and other high-level organizations like NATO and unified commands such as the Central Command.

The last and most prestigious military school is the Army War College or one of the comparable schools in the Department of Defense. Again, a board of generals sorts through the eligible officers' records and picks a small percentage of the brightest and best officers in the Army. These are the fastest of the "fast movers," and they will lead the Army in the years following their graduation. Some, like General H. Norman Schwarzkopf, will have their names on the front pages of every newspaper in the country.

In addition to the normal professional military education system, the Army also sends selected officers to civilian universities to obtain needed specialties that are beyond the Army education system's capability. These positions are extremely limited, as they are very expensive, and selection for civilian schooling, especially in the early sixties, was another signal that the Army was smiling on an officer and his career.

The advanced course at Fort Benning, Georgia to which Captain Schwarzkopf reported in 1961 was considered a "permanent change of station"—it was a real move and not just temporary duty. On permanent changes of station the officer is authorized to have his family and household goods moved at government expense. Being a bachelor at the time, this was not a factor affecting Schwarzkopf, but his marital status probably caused some good-natured kidding, as well as providing ever-present matchmakers with a wonderful project.

Somehow the government's reimbursement for moving a family has never matched the actual costs, so officers and men end up paying the difference out of their own pockets. While the carefree and wily bachelor captain wasn't concerned about family moving expenses, a future Mrs. Schwarzkopf would be. With permanent moves occurring every two or three years (and sometimes more often), a career officer and his family could expect anywhere from ten to fifteen moves in a twenty-year career. A military family moving into a civilian neighborhood can usually be identified because the wife has boxes of drapes and curtains for ten different houses. It's a nomadic life, but officers and their families get used to it—or get out.

For all but the few who are aiming for honor graduate status, the advanced course offers a much appreciated break from the ever stressful life in an active unit. An officer could do quite well in class and still have time to spend with his family, often after having spent over half his time away from home. There is time to renew old friendships in your branch, to swap stories about how hard it was at Fort "X" or who had the worst boss. Branch schools offer good training, but the opportunity for an officer to learn from his fellow students is equally important. It is a good time to learn, to relax with family, and to put career and personal goals in perspective.

Overall, Army training at the advanced level is an excellent system that serves the needs of both the Army and the individual.

It was in the supportive atmosphere of the Infantry Officers Advance Course that Norman spent a year, and then he received word that he had been selected for a real plum: advanced education at a civilian university. From Georgia, he moved to the University of Southern California, where he received his master's degree in mechanical engineering—quite unusual for an airborne infantry officer.

The Army wasn't about to spend that kind of money just so Captain Schwarzkopf could hang a diploma on his wall. So when he graduated, he was assigned to West Point as an instructor in mechanical engineering. But he only taught there for a year—it was 1965 and the Vietnam buildup had begun. The Army needed combat leaders more urgently than it needed mechanical engineers, and it didn't have far to look. There was a bear at West Point.

3

THE FIRST WAR—
THE BEST YEAR

To understand General Schwarzkopf, you must first understand the Army; but to understand today's Army it is essential to appreciate how it, its soldiers, and its attitudes were affected by the Vietnam experience. If the war was a trauma for the country, it was even more so for the soldiers who fought there—not only because of the combat, but because of what the Vietnam experience did to their Army and to their nation. Virtually every colonel and general in the Army today served at least one tour in Vietnam, and the experience is burned into their minds. The memory is so strong that it has been institutionalized and become a part of the system. The captains, majors, and lieutenants colonels who entered the service after Vietnam absorbed, and then spread the impressions they picked up from seniors they admired. Every army studies its past for lessons learned, and these are normally presented as part of the professional education system. But the lessons of the Vietnam War, perceived as well as actual, are not restricted to the classroom or professional journals. At least as important is their dissemination through what might be called the tribal system. At formal and informal meetings, at parties, or over a beer or a cup of coffee, the Vietnam experience is passed down from seniors to juniors. Some of this might be dismissed as just the spinning of war stories, but much of it isn't that, because it focuses on what "they"—self-seeking politicians and an indifferent public—did to the Army. Young volunteers and old professionals still deeply resent what happened to the Army in Vietnam and the years immediately following.

Norman Schwarzkopf is typical. In 1965, after four demanding years at West Point and nine years of arduous duty as an infantry junior officer, he was proud of his nation, his army, and his own accomplishments. He had chosen a profession that expected him to sacrifice his life on demand. He looked upon his profession not as that of one who killed, but rather as that of one who protected his fellow citizen. The motto, "Duty-Honor-Country" was not just words, but a way of life. He wasn't in the policy-making branch of the government. His role was to carry out the orders of his superiors as given to them by the country's elected officials. His government said the Republic of South Vietnam was under attack from North Vietnam and that the United States was going to the aid of a beleaguered democracy. Sure, he had heard protesters claim that the North Vietnamese were not involved and that the United States was interfering in a peasant revolt, but he knew better. To him the young protesters of 1965 appeared to be just a privileged few who were really only worried about being drafted. He dismissed them, going to Vietnam with a sense of honor and pride to do his duty for his country.

The newly promoted Major Schwarzkopf was assigned as an adviser to the elite Vietnamese Airborne, one of the best, toughest, and most dangerous assignments at the time. It was an unusual and often frustrating experience for a man who had trained all his career for command to find himself in the almost powerless position of an adviser.

There were advisers all over Vietnam; some were staff advisers, while others were field advisers.

Staff advisers worked with the Vietnamese staff officers at various levels, but usually did not live with them or go into combat with Vietnamese units. (It is impossible to picture the young, hard-charging Major Schwarzkopf as a staff adviser at some headquarters.)

The field adviser, on the other hand, was a member of the Vietnamese unit. He lived, slept, ate, fought, and sometimes died with his Vietnamese soldiers. To keep from being too conspicuous during firefights, he even wore their uniform, with its beret and distinctive unit insignia. It doesn't take much imagination to picture how well the six-feet, three-inch tall Major Schwarzkopf blended in as he moved among the five-feet, three-inch Vietnamese: a (probably not so jolly) Green Giant, among the pea pods. It could only have been luck and poor Viet Cong marksmanship that kept the future "Norman of Saudi Arabia" from being shipped home in an aluminum casket. (In fact, shortly after joining his Vietnamese unit, Schwarzkopf found himself cut off and surrounded by the enemy for several days.)

Living, working, and fighting with the Vietnamese gave Schwarzkopf a chance to obtain a unique insight into the culture of Vietnam, and a real perspective on the progress of the war. Before the arrival of large numbers of American units, field adviser positions with Vietnamese were assignments much sought after by officers eager to be where the action was. Norm was one of those officers.

The level of professionalism and training varied widely in the Vietnamese Army, and the adviser's role and duties varied from unit to unit and commander to commander. Over time the Army developed a bureaucracy to manage the advisory program, but down in the unit, where it really counted, it was always guys like Schwarzkopf who made the difference.

Unfortunately, in 1965 many Vietnamese officers couldn't speak English very well, and hardly any advisers could speak Vietnamese. Each three- or four-man battalion adviser team was assigned an interpreter, but even with a good interpreter it was hell trying to communicate in the thick of battle. In late 1965, the Army organized two courses, and every adviser was supposed to attend one of them. At Monterey, California, the prospective adviser would spend three months learning Vietnamese. The course at Fort Bragg, North Carolina, ran for only six weeks. There soldiers learned something of Vietnam and were introduced to a smattering of Viet Cong tactics and weapons. They also came away with a 500-word vocabulary of Vietnamese, naturally starting with the phrase, "Where are the VC?" An officer graduating from the course was termed a "Military Assistance Training Adviser," for which the acronym "MATA" was coined. (Immediately, some officer student claimed that the acronym really stood for "Mill Around 'Till Ambushed.")

Few prospective advisers really knew if they could actually eat dog, monkey, or snake meat if that were placed in front of them. Schwarzkopf did and became proud of the fact that he lived as the Vietnamese soldiers did, including eating their food. Advisers who didn't lost credibility and established little rapport with their Vietnamese counterparts.

"Rapport" was the Army's favorite buzz word in the advisory business, but it was interpreted differently by different people. Some advisers ignored deficiencies in their units in the interest of "rapport," but it's hard to visualize Stormin' Norman doing that. Schwarzkopf established his rapport by respecting the Vietnamese and getting them to respect him. He saw his job as getting the unit to do the best job it could in combat, trying to improve its effectiveness, controlling U.S. artillery and air support, and personally demonstrating America's commitment to South Vietnam. It would have been much easier had he exercised any real authority, but he didn't. And yet the U.S. Army held him responsible for how well the Vietnamese unit performed. A little ditty favored by advisers pretty much summed up how they viewed their job:

We're not allowed to run the train,
Or even toot the whistle,

But if the damn thing jumps the track,
We know who gets the missile!

Still, the adviser had one very great incentive
to improve his Vietnamese unit, even if it destroyed rapport with his counterpart: It might
cost him his life if the unit did poorly in combat.

★

Despite some of what has been said about the
South Vietnamese Army, many of its officers
were very good, very dedicated, and very professional. Advisers like Norm Schwarzkopf learned
a great deal from them and profited from the
experience. But regardless of what advisers
thought of their particular counterpart, few of
them failed to develop a certain affection for the
rank-and-file soldier. Exposed daily to the threat
of death and mutilation, living in conditions that
would appall a slum landlord, with little of what
we would call food, and poor pay, he usually did
his duty. Cheerful and always thrilled to talk to
an American, the Vietnamese infantryman was
as good a soldier as any when well led. Today
General Schwarzkopf is quick to say that he
considers that year in South Vietnam one of his
best tours of duty. Advising a good unit that was
well led by a commander who accepted good
advice was a very rewarding experience.

There were benefits to being an adviser in the

field, the best being the freedom. There were few superiors looking over Norm Schwarzkopf's shoulder, no one continually watching and evaluating what he did. The advisory teams were small and often far from the "flagpole" where individual initiative counted the most. Never before in his career had Schwarzkopf enjoyed so much latitude, and he would never have that kind of latitude again.

Another advantage was the insight he acquired with respect to other people. Iran had been interesting and so had Germany, but in Vietnam he was completely immersed in an alien culture. Norm found he could adapt and this experience, too, would serve him well in the Persian Gulf.

Since the very beginning of Operation Desert Shield, the international press has focused on Stormin' Norman's colorful nickname. The name is catchy, but it belies the experience of a man who has learned the fine art of diplomacy and persuasion in dealing with others of a different culture. Had Norman really been so "stormin'" he would never have been successful in getting a dozen different armies and twice that number of nationalities to follow his command.

During his year-long tour with the Vietnamese Airborne, he was wounded in action and decorated for gallantry in combat. When Major Schwarzkopf left Vietnam in mid-1966, America had suffered less than 7,000 men killed in action. Exactly three years later Lieutenant Colonel Schwarzkopf would return to the same country, but to a different army and a different war.

Once again assigned to the United States Military Academy, this time as an Associate Professor, Major Schwarzkopf buckled down to adjusting to a new environment and a new job. Going from the jungles of Vietnam to the Plains of West Point was a considerable change, and many might have thought he should have been assigned to a regular infantry unit, where his combat experience could be applied. But the Army knows that seeds are at least as important as the crop. Despite the ivy-covered walls and the classrooms, the purpose of the United States Military Academy is to turn bright young people into officers for the Army. Qualified, highly decorated officers who have been effective in battle provide valuable role models for the future officers corps.

Academics are important, but many of the young men (and now women) choose West Point because they want to be officers, not scholars. The young man who might be considering becoming a combat arms officer can't help but be impressed by a "professor" wearing the Combat Infantryman Badge, American and Vietnamese jump wings, a Purple Heart, and two Silver Stars! Being lectured to by someone wearing all those decorations and standing over six feet tall, probably insured an unusual amount of student attention in the Department of Mechanics. Major Schwarzkopf had been to the place that was getting all the headlines, the place where someday they'd be sent. He could tell them a lot more than just how to draw a straight line—he could tell them about Vietnam.

Schwarzkopf's tour at the Academy lasted from June 1966 to June 1968. When he had left Vietnam there had been less than 180,000 Americans there. By the end of 1967 that number had grown to 485,000, and U.S. death count had reached 16,000. Many changes were taking place both in Vietnam and at home. When Major Schwarzkopf had returned to the States, the antiwar movement was still comparatively small and a majority of Americans still supported the Administration. But Vietnam had begun to dominate the consciousness of the nation. Who better could the West Point cadets find to answer their questions than a man who had been in the thick of it and survived? It was only natural that the cadets would want his opinion of what was happening, and surely he could explain what was happening.

The young major must have gotten a boost to his ego from all the admiring young cadets. But how could he explain the 100,000 demonstrators who marched in New York in April? What could he say about the 50,000 who massed at the Pentagon in October? Most ominous of all, a poll published the following March showing that for the first time, more Americans opposed than supported the war. The Military Academy taught cadets that their army was the nation's—the people's—army. Were the people now abandoning their own soldiers? The perception that they were would leave lasting deep wounds on the Army. Even today, more than twenty-five years after the war, interviewers ask General Schwarzkopf how he and Operation Desert Storm were affected by Vietnam—and, with fire in his eyes, he will tell them. It remains the worst thing this country has ever done to its soldiers . . . and to itself. Even in the tremendous euphoria and pride generated by the defeat of Iraq, Vietnam is there—for Norm Schwarzkopf, his soldiers, the United States military—for everyone.

4

THE FIRST WAR—THE WORST YEAR

Despite his cadets' questions about Vietnam, not even Major Schwarzkopf could be a role model or think deep thoughts twenty-four hours a day. He was a young man and a bachelor, and New York City wasn't very far away. His teaching duties allowed him to have a normal social life, which soon focused on one person: Brenda Holsinger a beautiful and intelligent TWA flight attendant.

When they were married on July 6, 1968, Norm discovered that he had unintentionally followed an old Army rule: lieutenants can't marry (no time or money), captains may marry (some time and some money), and majors must marry (good for their careers). The newly married couple would soon be on their way to Fort Leavenworth, Kansas. To no one's surprise, Norm had been selected, a year ahead of his peers, for promotion to Lieutenant Colonel and attendance at the Command and General Staff College.

Fort Leavenworth is a small, but scenic old former frontier post, rich in history, and atmosphere. So it was a great place for a newly married Army couple to begin their life together. Since most of the students are married, Fort Leavenworth has an active, but informal social life where old friends get together and new friends are made. For the new wife, it is a wonderful, if perhaps a bit deceptive, introduction to Army life. Although more academically challenging than the Advance Course, officers can spend time with their families, despite the nightly study grind. Most of the officers in a given class are contemporaries, people who have been in the Army about the same length of time, so Norm already knew many of his classmates.

When the list of those who have been chosen for the next year's class is published, it generates a wave of emotion throughout the Army. Norm's joy at having been selected was tempered by the knowledge that some of the names he read had already appeared on weekly Vietnam casualty lists.

Most of the students in Norm's class already

wore combat ribbons, but all knew that they
probably would be going back to Vietnam after
they graduated in June. The Tet offensive had
triggered another big buildup of American
forces.

At civilian universities, students study what
others have done. At the Command and General
Staff College, some of what the students studied
was what they themselves had done—their battles, their successes, and their failures. Out of
class, they also discussed their government's pol-
icies—the "Graduated Response" policy the military was made to follow in Vietnam was given
an "F" by all the students. The officers were
upset because they believed America should either go in with massive force and get the job
done quickly, or not go in at all. The President
was acting like the woman who couldn't bear to
cut off her dog's tail, so she compromised by
nipping it off an inch at a time. Twenty-two years
later another President didn't make Norm
Schwarzkopf do that. As General Schwarzkopf
said to a CBS interviewer in 1990, "When you
are putting American lives on the line, don't
namby-pamby around and cause yourself to take
more casualties."

Other issues were also discussed, but in 1969,
a real moral bombshell hit the Army. It was a
letter written by a former infantryman. In it he
said that on March 16, 1968, U.S. soldiers of

Company C, 1st Battalion, 220th Infantry, of the American Division, had slaughtered 150 unarmed Vietnamese civilians.

There were long investigations, and several courts-martial, but most Army officers believed that the guilty parties were not all being punished, and that the sentences being handed down were not strong enough. How could so many mid- and high-level officers not have known what had happened? Why did it take a letter from a former draftee to bring the incident to light? What had happened to integrity?

Other things about the Army nagged at Schwarzkopf and other relatively junior officers. Too many officers and men in the base camps were living the "good life," while the grunts in the jungle picked leeches from their skin, ate cold rations, and lived in constant fear. The riflemen didn't like the short straw they had drawn, but could accept it. What they couldn't accept were the air-conditioned trailers, cheap booze, and party girls that many people enjoyed in the areas to the rear.

As if that weren't enough, they had to put up with senior officers who liked to "chopper" out to the jungle after a good night's sleep to check on the war. When they found something interesting or a good firefight, they would begin circling high overhead and start radioing orders or advice to the junior commander on the ground.

Sometimes there would be as many as four or five of these officers circling over a poor captain or lieutenant trying to fight the Viet Cong. General Schwarzkopf himself dates the start of his legendary temper to just such an incident in 1970. However, it's more likely that his change in temper was the result of his entire Vietnam experience.

In the second half of the Command and General Staff course, Lieutenant Colonel Schwarzkopf received his orders. Upon graduation in June 1969, he would again ship out to Vietnam—the same month that President Nixon announced he was withdrawing 25,000 American soldiers.

Eleven months after their wedding, Brenda Schwarzkopf watched her husband go off to war, for what would be their first, but not their last war separation.

★

For the few officers lucky enough to get the opportunity, commanding a battalion in combat is the job they will always remember most vividly. Command at any level is what every good officer wants, but the battalion is the largest unit that actually closes with and fights the enemy. Infantry or armor battalion commanders are leaders first and managers second. Commanders of higher-level units (brigades, divisions, corps, and so on) are more managers than leaders.

Competition for battalion command is intense because there are many more lieutenant colonels than there are battalions. Today, the Army does everything it can to make certain that only the best-qualified get battalions, and it only picks from its brightest and best officers, but that was not always the case in Vietnam.

Command in combat is an intense and exhausting job. It is also a personally and professionally dangerous one. Only one mistake—too many casualties, or walking on the wrong side of a tree—can kill the officer or his career. Battalion commanders get burned out or reach a point where they have pushed their luck far enough. When they finally give up command, they always look back, but almost never voluntarily *go back*.

Although the Vietnam conflict built up slowly, the Army was hard pressed to keep up with the need for good qualified people. It was forced to promote officers and men faster than it wanted. After the first couple of years of the war, the Army ran out of experienced people. Officers were promoted to captain after only two years, and then given a hundred-plus men to command in combat. Six months after leaving high school, a nineteen-year-old boy might find himself a sergeant trying to lead a ten-man squad. Unfortunately, it was the same for lieutenant colonels,

colonels, and generals. At the height of war, the Army was doing its best in Vietnam, but in many was as amateur force, much different from the Army Norm had left in 1966. And worst of all, it was becoming a demoralized army.

★

Lieutenant Colonel Schwarzkopf knew all this, but tried to put it out of his mind as he reported to Vietnam. As a young, but experienced hotshot, he figured he could make at least some difference. The chief of staff of the United States Army, Vietnam (USARV) thought so, too, because he grabbed Norm to be his executive officer.

Good "grunts" hate all staff jobs, but they hate some more than others. Despite the impressive title, an executive officer is rather like an executive secretary: You have no real power, but you know what is going on.

As much as he might have hated sitting behind a desk, the five months Schwarzkopf spent at USARV headquarters not only gave him the opportunity to see the big picture, but also to pick up information that might prove useful later when he finally got his battalion.

The big picture had really changed from the last time Norm had been in Vietnam. "Vietnamization" was in; U.S. forces were on their way out. Two months after he arrived in country, the U.S. 9th Infantry Division began withdrawing from Vietnam. Three months later, the 3d Marine Division pulled out, quickly followed by elements of the Army's 82d Airborne Division. The message to the rifleman in the jungle was *not* that he was going home early, but that he wouldn't be replaced when he left. The policy was quickly summed up in the advisory, "Don't be the last man killed in the war."

In December 1969, Norm cleared his desk, grabbed his helmet, and took command of the 1st Battalion, 6th Infantry, in the American Division's 198th Infantry Brigade. It was a very proud moment, and the start of what he was certain would be a rewarding experience . . . but that isn't how it turned out.

The American Division was not formed in the States, but put together on the battlefield. (Officially it was the Army's 23d Infantry Division, but until the My Lai massacre it was always called "American.") In 1967, the Army merged several brigades that had been operating in Vietnam, combining them to form a division. The same thing had been done in World War II in the Pacific. That division was called "American," a contraction of "Americans in New Caledonia." When the Army followed that precedent in Vietnam, it decided to use that same name.

The Vietnam American was a big division,

with eleven battalions of light infantry, an armored cavalry squadron (the same as a battalion), two armored reconnaissance troops (companies), an air reconnaissance troop, and six battalions of artillery. In addition, the division had three-plus battalions of its own assault helicopters and gunships. It was a very potent force.

In the media the Americal Division will always be tarnished by the actions of a few soldiers at My Lai. Ignored is the fact that most Americal soldiers fought cleanly and bravely. They won eleven Medals of Honor and suffered over 17,000 casualties, more than four times as many as the division had suffered in World War II.

As the battalion commander, Lieutenant Colonel Schwarzkopf commanded a unit that had great firepower and mobility, and he quickly perfected his talents for coordinating both to good advantage. Now, when being interviewed by reporters, he seldom mentions things like that. Instead he repeatedly refers to the morale and leadership problems then affecting his battalion and the rest of the Army, problems that started at the top and cascaded downward. As an old Chinese proverb puts it, "The head of the fish rots first."

He was disgusted by the easy living enjoyed by staff and support people in the rear areas. That made him so angry that he refused to go there unless expressly ordered to do so. Traditionally, front-line troops have always had a certain contempt for support troops in the rear. In Vietnam it grew so bad that the grunts coined a derisive new word, "REMF," which stood for "Rear echelon motherf-----." Deservedly or not, everyone in the rear became the object of the combat soldier's rage—REMFs became more hated than the Viet Cong.

The lack of caring that some had for the grunt angered Norm Schwarzkopf more than anything, and he began to grow more bad-tempered. Years later, when asked why he was called "Stormin' Norman," he mentioned an episode in Vietnam to illustrate how his reputation began. One of his soldiers had been wounded, and Norm was trying to get a medical evacuation chopper to get the man to a hospital. When none could get there in time, he tried to get a chopper orbiting overhead to take the soldier out. The pilot radioed back that he couldn't—he had a load of VIPs. When Schwarzkopf heard that he blew up, yelling obscenities into the radio microphone for all to hear. His outburst shocked the VIPs and others who were listening in the rear, but his own troops loved him for it. Word quickly got around that Norm had been willing to offend a bunch of high-ranking officers and risk being relieved of command and all for a lowly combat soldier. (A regular med-evac chopper came for the wounded man.)

General Schwarzkopf claims to hate his nickname, but one has to wonder if that is really so. Schwarzkopf has a reputation for awesome outbursts, but the explosions are almost always the result of someone's not doing his job or not adequately supporting front-line soldiers. One officer who had worked for General Schwarzkopf commented, "You think you been chewed out? Let me tell you—when Stormin' Norman gets done with you, you'll think that you were born with a tail!" He's quick to anger, but he is equally quick to apologize if it later turns out he was wrong. As he said in one interview, he wears his heart on his sleeve.

★

Besides a deterioration in the attitude and ethics of some—*but not all*—officers in Vietnam, Schwarzkopf was bothered by many other things. He was bothered by the "numbers game" forced on the military by the politicians. Body count numbers were easily cranked into computers, but did they really measure how the war was going? No one on the ground believed they did, but the "numbers crunchers" wanted them, and the politicians wanted lots of them. Soon the whole thing was out of hand, a macabre system of lies, distasteful to Schwarzkopf and every other conscientious officer. That is why every military officer who briefed reporters during Desert Storm adamantly refused to talk about the number of Iraqi soldiers that had been killed.

Later General Schwarzkopf said, "Carelessness, negligence, lousy leadership, and self-serving officers and generals . . . people who are more concerned with their ambition than with their troops . . . cost human lives." The people indicated in that comment are the ones who truly feel General Schwarzkopf's fury.

Lieutenant Colonel Schwarzkopf's tour as a combat battalion commander was unhappy because of what the Army had become, and because the war was terrible. One of the worst incidents that happened to him put him in the public spotlight long before he became a national hero. One of his men was accidentally killed by friendly artillery. Regrettably, there have been "friendly fire" casualties in every war, and there will be more in the future. But this particular incident produced newspaper articles, television reports, a book, and finally a television movie.

When Sergeant Michael E. Mullen's parents asked how their son had been killed, the fumbling Army bureaucracy handled the situation very poorly. The result was that Mrs. Mullen made her anger public. The inept handling of this one incident at the time seemed to reflect the Army's general incompetence and indifference, so the press pushed the story hard.

Author C. D. B. Bryan investigated the story and wrote a best-selling book titled *Friendly Fire*. In it he was rightfully critical of the Army, but praised Lieutenant Colonel Schwarzkopf as a competent commander who showed compassion and concern for his soldiers. Unfortunately, like the Americal Division, Schwarzkopf's name became linked with the Mullen incident. Those who actually read the book came to admire him, but others automatically linked the name "Schwarzkopf" with the term "friendly fire."

On May 28, 1970, one of Schwarzkopf's companies stumbled into a Viet Cong minefield. Several men were wounded, including the company commander and a platoon leader. Landing his helicopter, Schwarzkopf immediately took charge and began to have the men carefully retrace their footsteps to safety. Unfortunately, one of the soldiers stepped on another mine, seriously wounding him and lightly wounding Schwarzkopf. Despite his own injuries, Schwarzkopf moved forward to help the man. Then another mine went off, killing three men and seriously wounding a fourth. Schwarzkopf continued to work his way around the minefield until all his men were finally safe. It was this incident, not any hastily presumed responsibility for misdirected friendly fire, that showed the true H. Norman Schwarzkopf. (Schwarzkopf was awarded his third Silver Star medal for his bravery in this situation.)

Six weeks later Lieutenant Colonel Schwarzkopf's tour was finished. He was on his way home to Brenda and to an Army that needed fixing.

5

★ ★ ★ ★

"POLISHING"

From the frustration and confusion of the Vietnam jungles, Schwarzkopf returned to the frustration and confusion of the Pentagon. In Vietnam, Norm's workday was twenty-four hours; in Washington, it was only a bit less. A lieutenant colonel's salary didn't go very far in the capital, so he and Brenda had to find a cheaper place to live. The long commute meant less time at home with his wife and new daughter, Cindy.

Most officers realize that a tour of duty in Washington is essential if they ever hope to be promoted to general. However, few really want to go there. To be offered an assignment at the Department of the Army or Department of Defense level means the Army regards you as a "comer." It is great for the ego, awful on the pocketbook, and more than a little humiliating. Lieutenant colonels are powerful men in battalions, but have little stature in the Pentagon. Yet, just as basic training makes a civilian into a soldier, the Pentagon experience polishes a rough field officer. Over the twenty years following his return from Vietnam, Schwarzkopf pulled *four* tours at the Pentagon. Despite his plain talk and sometimes crusty mannerisms, Norm Schwarzkopf became very polished indeed.

Schwarzkopf's first job in Washington wasn't really in what the Army calls the "Puzzle Palace," where everyone tries to fit his or her piece of the military puzzle into place. His department's mission was to see that officers were educated and trained, and then to fit them into assignments. He was to be in charge of the professional development of junior and mid-level infantry officers. He was responsible for making certain the right officers for necessary training were picked at the right time in their careers.

While Schwarzkopf was busy assigning young officers, other "Young Turks" at the War College were busy evaluating the Army. When their report, titled "Study on Military Professionalism," was released, it caused a sensation. Candid and devastatingly critical, it blasted the lack of leadership and professionalism within the Army's officer corps. The colonels and lieutenant colonels bluntly told the generals that they didn't like what had been going on and that the Army had to change.

Allegedly on the orders of the Army Chief of Staff, access to the study was immediately restricted to only generals. However, like everything else in Washington, it was soon leaked, and before long many lesser-rank officers were reading it. It was only the first shot in what would become a kind of guerilla war, but the young colonels were confident of eventual victory. After all, they had been taught how to fight a guerilla war by experts. Officers like Schwarzkopf were going to change the Army whether any of the old generals liked it or not. In fact, many of the generals, particularly those wearing one and two stars, agreed with all or at least parts of the report.

★

After only two years in Washington, Schwarzkopf was notified that he had been selected to attend that same hotbed of dissent: the U.S. Army War College, at Carlisle Barracks, Pennsylvania. As noted earlier, only a small fraction of officers is picked for the War College. His selection was a strong signal that he probably would be promoted to full colonel, and that he was in the running for selection to command a brigade. It also meant that he was in the ever-shrinking group of candidates for ultimate promotion to general. And then Brenda gave him more good news: Another baby (a girl, later named Jessica) was on the way.

★

The Army War College is situated at historic old Carlisle Barracks, a military facility dating from the Revolutionary War. It is so small that all of the institution is within walking distance of the students' homes.

The course, sometimes referred to as "the best year of your life," lives up to its billing. Students may wear civilian clothes to classes, seminar groups of from ten to fifteen men. Instruction from the podium is held to a minimum in favor of informal, round-table discussions. The topics are national and international in scope, and the instructors are very professional. Experts on every imaginable subject are invited as guest speakers. The atmosphere is relaxed and designed to stimulate interest.

In Schwarzkopf's day the War College was a gentlemen's course, and correctly labeled as education, not training. All the students were what the Army called "heavy hitters." Everyone knew that within the student body were the Army's future generals, a few of whom might someday command large armies in battle.

When the course ended in 1973, Norm Schwarzkopf had only been away from the troops for three years. He should have gone back to the Pentagon or to another high-level staff job. After a short Pentagon stint he got the job of Deputy Commander of the 172d Infantry Brigade, in Alaska.

To officers who worked hard to get all their "tickets punched," this didn't appear to be a smart move. No *smart* officer leaves the corridors of power to go off to someplace as far from the Pentagon flagpole as Alaska. Yet it was a good move, because the two years he spent there were invaluable preparation for his next posting. In October 1976, the now full Colonel H. Norman Schwarzkopf was given command of the 1st Brigade, 9th Infantry Division, at Fort Lewis, Washington. He didn't have to waste time learning the job. He was a fully qualified brigade commander the instant the brigade's flag was handed to him. He knew what had to be done and he knew how to do it.

In the military, each level of command has its own characteristics and requires a different approach. In the Army, the battalion is a fighting *unit*, while the brigade is a command and control *headquarters*. The only soldiers permanently assigned to a brigade are those few needed to operate the headquarters. When the division gives the brigade a mission, the brigade commander decides how he will accomplish it with his battalions. Then the brigade staff works out a plan, the commander approves it, and it is given to the battalion commanders to carry out. Battalion commanders do the same thing. They get the brigade commander's order and then decide what their companies must do to accomplish the mission. The process is the same throughout the entire chain of command. The commander at each level is responsible to his boss for what his subordinate commanders do. In this sense, Schwarzkopf's responsibilities were no different from those he had as platoon leader. Except now he had over 2,000 men under him instead of forty.

As big as this change was, it was nothing compared to what was happening in the Army. Most of the "old guard" had retired, replaced by "Young Turks" who were determined to have a healthy fighting force again. A Congressionally imposed reduction in strength had flushed substandard officers from the service. (In fact, the manpower cuts were so big that the Army had to release thousands of officers it would have liked to keep.) The draft had been abolished and now only volunteers joined. Every procedure and technique was analyzed to see what changes had to be made. Doctrine and tactics were studied, changed, and then studied again. The organizational sickness had been stopped, and the Army was getting healthy again.

In 1978, Colonel Schwarzkopf turned over the brigade and headed to Hawaii, but not for a vacation. He was to become the Deputy Director for Plans in the U.S. Pacific Command, his first "joint" assignment.

The Army does *not* fight wars, and neither does the Air Force or the Navy. The *military* fights them—that is, they all fight *jointly*. As one recent article put it, America's wars are fought by "barons of battle," the commanders of the Defense Department's unified commands. One general or admiral is appointed commander-in-chief (CINC), and the commanders of the service (Army, Navy, Air Force) components work directly for him. The CINC commands them and in turn they command the forces their services have provided to the unified command.

However, until a few years ago the idea of unified commands didn't work very well in practice. There was too much inter-service rivalry, and the Chairman of the Joint Chiefs of Staff was more of a chairman of the board than the President's senior military commander. Service component commanders frequently went around their CINC and complained to their own service chief when they didn't like something.

In 1978, getting a punch in a ticket printed

"joint duty" wasn't much good. It was interesting to work with officers of other services, but it really didn't help an ambitious officer's career. Congress was angry with the services for spending more time fighting each other than planning to fight an enemy, but hadn't forced any real changes.

Schwarzkopf charged into his new assignment with the same determination that he had displayed in all the other jobs he had done. He did good work and impressed the Navy officers with his cooperation and willingness to learn about their problems. (He probably also impressed them with his ability to chew out people who made mistakes.) He also found there was more to war than an attacking infantry division being supported by Air Force fighter bombers. Although he didn't realize it at the time, he had just taken a big step toward becoming a battlefield baron.

★

Norm Schwarzkopf wasn't "Norm" any more; he was "General" Schwarzkopf. To few people's surprise the Army gave him a star to put on his collar, a red general's flag to put behind his desk, and a fancy belt to put around his ample waist. It also sent him and his family (including a new son named Christian) to Europe. There, in August 1980, he took over as assistant division commander of the 8th Mechanized Infantry Division.

Divisions are commanded by major generals who have two brigadier general assistants. One assistant division commander looks after the tactical side of things, while the other is responsible for logistics. The new General Schwarzkopf got the logistics job, usually considered the less desirable of the two. Not only did he find himself in a new field, he found himself in a new type of unit—a mechanized one. Airborne soldiers and straight "leg" infantrymen usually don't want anything to do with mech. Too much time and effort is spent working on the armored personnel carriers just to keep them running. Although they beat "humping" a hundred-pound rucksack, they go so fast that it's sometimes difficult to keep track of where one is on the map. As for logistics, only the rare bird likes that.

Naturally, General Schwarzkopf would never complain in public about the lack of glamour in his job, but somehow it's hard to visualize him enjoying it. Yet, however enjoyable it may or may not have been, it certainly came in handy in Saudi Arabia where logistics was his biggest problem, when preparing to fight with a mechanized force. He must have fulfilled his duties with his usual gusto, because the Army selected him for promotion to major general.

In August 1982, after two years of being an assistant division commander, General Schwarzkopf went back to the Pentagon to be the Army's director of military personnel management. He was back where he had worked ten years and three ranks before, but this time he was the big boss. However, almost before Brenda could get the pictures on the wall and the drapes hung in their new house, Norm was picked to command the 24th Mechanized Infantry Division. In June 1983, he arrived at Fort Stewart, Georgia, and accepted the division's flag as the symbol of his command.

In the old Vietnam days, commanders rarely retained command for more than six months, or occasionally a little longer. That was one of the major problems in the Army. In that short period, a commander had almost no time to learn his job and correct his unit's deficiencies. So the deficiencies just multiplied, and things got worse. Now, in 1983, the commander had time to get the job done properly. Major General Schwarzkopf would keep his 24th Mechanized Infantry Division for two years, polishing his logistics and mech skills. Yet, before he could really get into his new command, he was called away for a temporary job.

In the first major military action since Vietnam, President Reagan decided to invade Grenada. Given only a few days to plan, a joint task force was formed and directed to take the island on October 25, 1983. Unlike CENTCOM in Desert Storm, the task force for Operation Urgent Fury was an ad hoc organization. Vice Admiral Joseph Metcalf III was given command, and he needed a senior Army officer as a liaison officer. Norm Schwarzkopf was picked for the job because he had experience working with the Navy from his Pacific Command days. It was intended that Schwarzkopf be the Army liaison officer, but when he reported, Admiral Metcalf changed his duties. Metcalf made Norm the Deputy Task Force Commander.

Although successful, Urgent Fury revealed the many problems inherent in joint operations: communications, coordination, tactics, and so on. Grenada confirmed the criticisms the government's General Accounting Office had made in 1979. GAO report had reported that the services seldom took action to correct deficiencies discovered during joint training exercises.

Even after Grenada things hadn't improved much. In 1985, General Wallace Nutting, the commander-in-chief of the joint United States Readiness Command, conducted an unclassified study of joint exercises. After examining seventeen joint exercises, Nutting's task force identified major problems in command, control, and communications. Any second lieutenant knows that if you have problems in those areas, your unit is headed for defeat. With an IQ of 170, duty in a joint command, and experience with an actual joint shooting war, General Schwarzkopf knew the problems well.

★

After leaving the division in June 1985, Schwarzkopf spent another year in the Pentagon in the office of the Army's Deputy Chief of Staff for Operations. Not only was this one of the most prestigious offices in the Department of the Army, it was almost a guarantee of bigger things to come. In Norm Schwarzkopf's case that was promotion to lieutenant general and command of I Corps at Fort Lewis, Washington, in June 1986. He would have a year to sharpen his skills in commanding and controlling multi-divisional operations. Then it was back to the Pentagon for the fourth time.

In November 1988, General Schwarzkopf pinned on his fourth star, and became the Commander-in-Chief, U.S. Central Command. He didn't know it, but he had a year and nine months to work out the problems with joint operations. Then he would take the biggest military force the United States had assembled since Vietnam, and conduct the shortest and most successful war in the nation's history.

6

COMMAND

There was no big parade when General Schwarzkopf arrived in Florida to take over as Commander-in-Chief of the United States Central Command (CENTCOM). He didn't stand on a reviewing platform looking out over all the thousands of men he now comanded. The hair on the back of his neck didn't stand up as the colors (flags) of ten or twenty divisions dipped when the National Anthem was played. He didn't do those things because he really didn't command anything. All he had was a staff of a few hundred officers and men.

Like the other unified commands, CENTCOM was primarily a planning headquarters. In Europe, General John Galvin was the Commander-in-Chief (CINC) of the United States European Command, but he spent little time at his headquarters in Germany. He was too busy doing his full-time job as NATO's Supreme Allied Commander in Belgium. (The only time a CINC commands any real combat forces is during a joint exercise or in a war. He's only a "battlefield baron" when there is a battlefield.)

Unified commands spend most of their time rewriting contingency plans. The U.S. military has contingency plans for almost every area in the world. If Brazil and Argentina went to war over a soccer game, the Southern Command probably could find a contingency plan if the war threatened U.S. national interests.*

Making certain that all contingency plans are kept current is a lot of work. The world is always changing, and the staff officer in a unified command never quite catches up. It's interesting work, but a little frustrating when you know there is precious little chance that your plan will ever be needed.

It is also frustrating when the officers who really command forces (the guys who are *not* in unified commands) argue that their service doesn't agree with what you want. It takes a bull—or a bear—with a lot of determination to make the unified command idea work.

---

*Soccer wars have almost broken out before in Latin America, although not between these two countries.

Many things had happened in the five years since General Schwarzkopf and Admiral Metcalf had taken a joint task force into Grenada. Congress had forced the services to start working together better. Although Congress didn't change the title, it made the Chairman of the Joint Chiefs of Staff the actual boss. It told the services that if their officers wanted to get promoted to the higher-level ranks, they had better have "joint" duty. They also ordered the military to make the unified command a place where people worked hard, instead of going golfing on Friday afternoon. In short, Congress intended to make the CINCs almost as important in peacetime as they would be in war. Stormin' Norman had to have loved that idea.

Each unified command focuses on one region of the world. For example, the European Command's area is (naturally) Europe; Southern Command's is Latin America; and the Pacific Command covers the Pacific, including Korea and Southeast Asia. The Central Command focuses on someplace the U.S. military calls "Southwest Asia." Most atlases don't even show a "Southwest Asia," but it's the area around the Middle East. It's also a region that the United States likes to stay out of as much as possible, particularly with its ground forces.

The U.S. military has provided soldiers to United Nations peacekeeping forces in the Sinai and in Lebanon. It also has conducted joint exercises with the Egyptians, and occasionally with troops from other friendly nations in the area. However, most of the time we sail our ships well offshore.

When Norm Schwarzkopf took over, CENTCOM officers were watching and planning, but most never thought they would actually use the plans. After all those Marines were blown up in Beirut, it would have to be something really big before America would put troops on the ground anywhere in the Middle East.

★

Shortly after midnight on August 2, 1990, Iraq's Saddam Hussein launched a massive tank attack on Kuwait. By that evening Kuwait City was in his hands, and his 95,000 troops had overwhelmed tiny Kuwait's 20,000-man army. The attack was so swift that the first indication many Kuwaitis had that something had happened was when they saw Iraqi tanks in the streets.

It was just after noon in Florida when CENTCOM first got the news, and the word quickly spread through the headquarters. That evening some officers told their wives that they might have to go in to the office on the weekend.

As the United Nations Security Council met

in emergency session, CENTCOM was going over its contingency plans. Some were envious of Southern Command for having had so much time to prepare for the invasion of Panama. If the President decided to do anything more than send ships into the Persian Gulf, CENTCOM was going to have to hit the ground running.

At Fort Bragg, North Carolina, the XVIII Airborne Corps and the 82d Airborne Division had already been placed on alert. Elsewhere around the country and abroad, Air Force, Navy, and Marine Corps units had also gotten the word that they might need to move out.

By August 5, the Iraqi army was within ten miles of the Saudi border. Saddam Hussein had increased the number of troops in Kuwait to 150,000 men. He now had two tank, one mechanized, and three infantry divisions, with over 1,500 tanks and 750 artillery guns within range of Saudi oil fields.

Saudi Arabia was worried. With only 65,000 men, 550 tanks, and 189 combat aircraft, the country couldn't stand up to Saddam Hussein. The Saudis were already badly outnumbered, and Saddam Hussein still had *another* 850,000 men, 4,000 tanks, and 689 combat aircraft he could use. Saddam Hussein had invaded Kuwait to get oil, and Saudi Arabia had two-and-a-half times as much as Kuwait did. King Fahd needed

help immediately, so he turned to George Bush.*
President Bush turned to Defense Secretary Dick
Cheney, General Colin Powell—and Norman
Schwarzkopf.

---

*On the whole Saudi–U.S. relations have been very good
over the years. Because of Middle Eastern tensions, both governments prefer to keep quiet about it, but we actually have better
relations with the Saudis than with some of our nearer friends.

DESERT
SHIELD

7

A NIGHTMARE

On August 7, Saddam Hussein's one-million-man army was either in Kuwait or within a couple hundred miles of it. The United States' two million men and women in military service were scattered all over the globe. For example, on that Tuesday the U.S. Army had nine divisions training in the States, four in Germany, and one in Korea. It had battalions and brigades training in Honduras and Panama, fighting forest fires in the western United States, and supporting counter-narcotics operations. The Army actually had one battalion on the ground in the Middle East, but with the United Nations Peacekeeping Force in the Sinai. The Air Force, Navy, and

Marines were similarly deployed around the world.

When the President made the decision to send American troops to the Persian Gulf, he gave General Schwarzkopf two missions: Defend Saudi Arabia and "conduct other operations as directed." He also handed him a giant logistics headache, and started a seven-month nightmare for everyone involved.

Schwarzkopf and his component (Army, Navy, Air Force) commanders had to get some troops and firepower in Saudi Arabia immediately. They had to have at least some American soldiers along the northern Saudi border to make Saddam Hussein stop and think. He was used to U.S. rhetoric. Except for Panama and Grenada, which were really special cases, America was loath to back its words with military action. But Saddam Hussein *did* know that if his T-72 Soviet-made tanks rolled over American soldiers, the United States would come at him with a vengeance.

First on the troop list of most contingency plans is the 82d Airborne Division, at Fort Bragg, North Carolina. It is a well-trained division, filled with soldiers who know they're good. But they are not number one on the list just because they're good. They are there because the entire division and everything it owns can be loaded into C-141 jet transports and sent anywhere in the world within hours. If necessary, the airplanes don't even have to land. The load masters just open the doors and everyone jumps. There was no question or hesitation at CENTCOM. A week after Saddam Hussein invaded Kuwait, the Air Force began landing the 82d Airborne in Saudi Arabia.

While the Airborne could quickly set up a defensive line, it would be very thin on the ground and wouldn't have the heavy weapons needed to fight enemy armor. So Schwarzkopf told the Pentagon he also wanted U.S. Marines.

There was nothing macho about wanting paratroopers and Marines. The Marine Corps kept tanks, artillery, and heavy equipment loaded on "maritime prepositioning ships" (MPS). Within hours of receiving orders, the ships could get under way and begin sailing to the Persian Gulf. Most of the Marine "grunts" flew ahead to Saudi Arabia to meet the ships when they docked. The lead elements of the Marine Corps began arriving in country at the same time as the paratroopers.

Both the Marines and the Airborne were "light" units, without much armor or heavy weapons. CENTCOM needed to get Army "heavy" divisions into the theater. The two-brigade 24th Mechanized Infantry Division was stationed at Fort Stewart, near the port of Savannah, Georgia. It immediately began preparing its tanks and armored vehicles, and packing its equipment. By the end of the week the first of the Navy's SL-7 Fast Sealift ships began steaming into the Atlantic.

As the name implies, the SL-7 is a very fast ship, with "roll-on, roll-off" capability, meaning that it can quickly load and unload cargo. It could leave the east coast of the United States and make it to Saudi Arabia in two weeks, about twice as fast as a regular cargo ship. Unfortunately, Navy officers want to command combat ships, so there are only eight SL-7s in our "600-ship Navy." Because of the crisis, the Navy had to start chartering commercial vessels, and start pulling cargo ships out of mothballs. It took seven of the SL-7s and two charted cargo vessels to get just the 24th Mech Division to Saudi Arabia. Then the ships had to take a couple of weeks to return for more.

The tanks that the Marines were unloading were the older M60s. They were good and had been upgraded since they were first produced in the 1960s, but they could not technically match the more powerful Soviet-built T-72s. So the Army had designed and built the M1 Abrams tank, with a 105mm main gun and better armor. The "arms race" is much more than just building more and better ICBMs, so a few years later the M1 was modified. The M1A1 had a 120mm gun and better armor. It also had an on-board pressure system that could seal the crew inside and keep chemical agents from entering. Additionally, it had air conditioning, which would come in handy in the 115-degree desert heat.

Everything that made the M1 and M1A1 great tanks also made them very heavy. The giant Air Force C-5A transport plane could carry two Abrams tanks, but not all the way to the Persian Gulf. With the extra weight of the fuel the C-5A needed to fly long distances, it could only carry *one* tank. Flying heavy M1 and M1A1 tanks to Saudi Arabia was impractical and expensive, but it had to be done. CENTCOM, the Army, and the Marines couldn't fight Saddam Hussein's thousands of tanks without them.

While American civilians were glued to their television sets, Defense Department people (military and civilian) were frantically working twenty-four hours a day trying to keep up with everything.

For example, General Schwarzkopf would tell the Army that he needed an armored division in Saudi Arabia as soon as possible. The Army then notified a commander that his unit was the one. Since everyone in the Army had been told to start getting ready, that armored division had already done a lot of preparation. But because other units had priority, it hadn't been able to do everything. Now it began to get transporters (tractor trailers) to move its tanks and armored

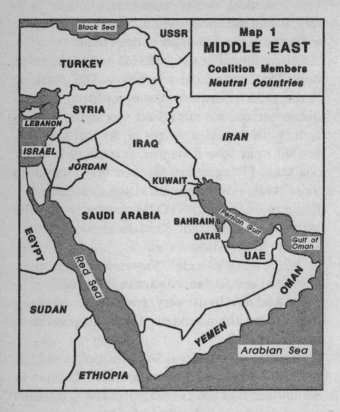

vehicles to the railhead or port. Enormous amounts of supplies and equipment had to be crated and loaded on trucks. If the vehicles were green camouflage, they had to be painted tan. If something was broken, it had to be fixed immediately. Troops had to be processed, shots given, wills prepared, dog tags checked, desert uniforms issued . . . and on and on. "Operation Desert Shield," as it was now being called, was an intense, high-speed, complicated nightmare.

On August 22, President Bush ordered a call-up of as many as 200,000 reservists and National Guardsmen. At first most people were stunned, because they thought the reserves were only called up in wartime. Later they found that much of the military's support services had been assigned to the reserves. The active duty military would not be able to use very much of its combat power without the reservists. Their use was the only way the United States could have an army big enough to fight a major war. We hadn't been caught short—it had been planned that way.

Within the first thirty days, more than 38,000 men and two divisions were in the Saudi desert, most of them brought by air. Over a 150,000 tons of weapons, vehicles, equipment, and supplies had arrived. At the end of sixty days the numbers had grown to more than a 100,000 troops, and a half-million tons of cargo—and the numbers kept climbing, right up to the end of the war.

Whole books will be written about just this
phase of Desert Shield, but the sheer magnitude
of the numbers is enough to overwhelm most
people.

General Schwarzkopf was ultimately responsible for the operation's going smoothly, but it
was a joint effort. The services were making the
"unified" concept work.

8

★ ★ ★ ★

WILL WE FIGHT?

From the moment President Bush announced
that he was sending American forces to Saudi
Arabia, the question was, "Will we really have to
fight the Iraqis?" Most thought no, but the answer was almost irrelevant to the military. It had
to assume that there would be war—it couldn't
afford to assume otherwise.

Norm Schwarzkopf was worried, maybe even
scared. If Saddam Hussein sent his tanks south,
a lot of young Americans were going to die. Good
military leaders feel about their men as parents
feel about their children. They have to guide
them, teach them, discipline them, and love
them—and sometimes they have to send them to
their death. It is an awesome responsibility that

few men are willing to accept. Schwarzkopf had accepted it before, and he didn't want to have to do it again. Neither did the leaders under him.

The first few weeks were the most critical. Somebody had said that the United States and its allies had "drawn a line in the sand," but it was an exceptionally thin one. In fact, it wasn't a line at all. Saddam Hussein had enough people to spread all across the front, but not General Schwarzkopf.

After the Vietnam war, the United States turned its attention back to Europe. There the Soviet Red Army and the Warsaw Pact armies were much stronger than those of the United States and its NATO allies. Even if NATO had wanted to build another Maginot Line, it couldn't; it didn't have enough soldiers.

After having some of its brightest people study the numbers problem, the U.S. Army developed the best solution it could: the "mobile defense." Platoons, companies, and battalions would deploy into positions on the reverse slopes of hills, the side away from the enemy. Our tanks would get just high enough on the hill to be able to poke their guns over the top. That way most of the tank was hidden behind the hill, and the enemy could only shoot at the smaller turret. The TOW missile launchers and other weapons would be deployed in the same manner.

As soon as the enemy started to attack, U.S.

forces would begin hitting him with long-range artillery and air strikes. As the enemy moved closer, more of our weapons would be in range and they would start shooting at him. When he got close enough, our tanks and TOW missiles would start firing.

Of course the enemy would be shooting back, but because of the intervening hill we would be harder to hit. At that point the enemy—the Soviets, in most planning scenarios—would have lost many tanks and armored vehicles, while we probably would have lost very few.

When the enemy got so close that he could start knocking out our tanks, we would quickly pull back to another hill behind us. Meanwhile, another American position set up just like the first, but a little farther back, would begin doing the same thing we had.

The various U.S. units would take turns leap-frogging back, one firing while the other moved. No unit was supposed to stay in position long enough to get into a real slugfest. The idea was to keep playing "cowboys and Indians" until the enemy had taken so many casualties that he would turn around and go back.

All the war games, field tests, and computer analyses pointed to this "mobile defense" as an effective way to fight when outnumbered and still have a good chance of winning. All our soldiers were trained in the technique and knew how to execute it. The NATO armies were ready and had the right equipment to fight the Warsaw Pact. Unfortunately, in Saudi Arabia there were almost no hills to hide behind, and the "mobile" defense lacked the needed mobility. Paratroopers and Marines moved on foot; they weren't mechanized.

Schwarzkopf and his Army and Marine field commanders, Lieutenant Generals John Yeosock and Walter Boomer, didn't have much choice. Until the supply ships returned with the Army's heavy mechanized and armored divisions, they'd just have to pray.

★

But Saddam Hussein didn't order his army south into Saudi Arabia. It was soon clear that Bush's decision to commit American troops had taken him completely by surprise. He had assumed that after he had taken Kuwait, the United States would talk tough but wouldn't bring itself to do anything that he couldn't handle. He soon realized that he had miscalculated, but at least he'd still keep Kuwait and its oil fields. The trade embargo imposed by the United Nations would ultimately start to leak, the Allies would begin to squabble, and the antiwar movement in America would force Bush to withdraw.

General Norman Schwarzkopf didn't have

much time to spend contemplating the big picture. He was only happy that American and Allied units were pouring into Saudi Arabia. As combat units arrived, he and his two ground commanders sent them north to fill holes in the line. The Air Force had more fighters and close air support planes, and additional Navy aircraft carrier groups had steamed within range. Each day the CENTCOM staff briefings were easier to listen to. The first few days after arriving in Riyadh had been hectic, but now the staff was functioning smoothly.

Air Force Lieutenant General Charles Horner had arrived in Saudi Arabia first, and had acted as temporary in-theater commander. When Schwarzkopf arrived, Horner moved back to what he liked doing best: commanding the Air Force component.

Schwarzkopf needed a deputy, somebody he already knew and who knew him. So he got on the telephone and asked for Lieutenant General Calvin Waller, who commanded the I Corps at Fort Lewis, Washington. General Waller, an outstanding officer (and an African-American), agreed, but asked to have his corps command back when Desert Shield was finished.

The Navy component commander, Vice Admiral Stanley Arthur was doing whatever Navy guys do. Few people in either the Army or the Air Force have ever quite come to grips with Naval operations and procedures. Fortunately Norm Schwarzkopf had, and he was happy with what the Navy was doing.

Schwarzkopf and Saudi General Khalid bin Sultan al-Saud seemed to get along very well, but even if they weren't, neither would give any hint of disagreement in public. Schwarzkopf clearly did like the tough-looking, red beret–wearing, submachine-gun-toting Saudi guards who had been assigned to guard him constantly. They were real soldiers.

Space in the underground command bunker was cramped. There were temporary partitions everywhere to help people concentrate on their particular assignments, but that's almost standard operating procedure in the military. The underground setup certainly beat a non-air-conditioned building above ground. Besides, there was Saddam Hussein's Scud.

★

The first part of the mission President Bush had given Schwarzkopf, to defend Saudi Arabia, appeared to have been accomplished. Now it was time to turn to the second part—"conduct other operations as directed." Since there was no intention of withdrawing from Saudi Arabia with the question of Iraqi aggression unresolved, that could only mean "attack." Bush demanded that

Iraq leave Kuwait, but in words that seemed intended to force Saddam Hussein to fight.

Like most dictators, Saddam Hussein had built a personality cult. His picture was everywhere in Iraq, and people clapped, cheered, and kissed his hand when he appeared in public. Of course it was very dangerous not to show enthusiasm. People Saddam Hussein found disagreeable or disloyal were frequently tortured to death. Saddam Hussein set himself up as a great leader, not just of the Iraqis, but of all Arabs. As such, he could not survive the humiliation of backing down to George Bush. It doesn't take an expert or a CIA analyst to know that a man like Saddam Hussein cannot show weakness. He couldn't take a loss of face. When Bush refused to offer any face-saving concession, rejected any behind-the-scenes negotiations, and publicly demanded that Saddam Hussein unconditionally get out . . . one could only conclude the President must have wanted Saddam to stay, to suffer getting his butt kicked.

Even if the President had told General Schwarzkopf nothing about what those "other operations as directed" were likely to be, Norm was smart enough to figure out there was going to be a fight. He had to get the troops ready.

★

Of all the wars America has fought, Desert Storm will be ranked as one of the best for intelligence. The Allies knew just about everything they needed to know about the Iraqi army. Naturally they expected a few surprises, but perfect knowledge is unachievable. The Allies knew the enemy's equipment (moderate to good quality), knew how the enemy defended itself and how they attacked (they followed Soviet strategies), and they knew what kind of fighters the Iraqis were (some good, the rest poor). The Allies had studied them for eight years during the Iran–Iraq war and knew as much about them as was known about the West's previous archenemy, the Soviet Red Army.

So when the Iraqis began digging in and building the "Saddam Line," the Americans began training for the attack. The engineers built replicas of Iraqi fortifications, and the troops practiced attacking them. The Allied troops had always trained in the United States and Europe to penetrate and destroy Soviet-style fortifications; the desert required a different approach. Detailed classes were given on Iraqi mines and booby traps, and then units were trained in how to clear minefields. Everyone practiced donning gas masks and protective clothing, but that wasn't new. The military had always done that, but now it was done with enthusiasm. Equipment was tested, broken, fixed, and then modified for the desert. Tanks and armored fighting vehicles roared across the desert, and jet aircraft practiced low-level flying over desert terrain. Then they practiced high-level bombing runs, because of all the anti-aircraft artillery the Iraqi army had. It took a while to get enough live ammunition in the theater to use in training, but once it arrived everyone began blasting away.* Special Forces teams were attached to all major Allied units to train them in our tactics. When the time came, they would coordinate with nearby American units, and control U.S. artillery and air support. In short, everyone trained to do his part in the new air-land battle doctrine.

★

On November 8, President Bush announced that he was doubling the number of U.S. troops in Saudi Arabia. Schwarzkopf already knew that was to happen. The people being added were the VII Corps, including the 1st and 3d Armor Divisions, and the 2d Armored Cavalry Regiment. This was a heavy *attack* force.

---

*Probably to conceal an ammunition shortage, it was said at first that the Saudi government was reluctant to approve firing live ammunition.

DESERT
STORM

9

★ ★ ★ ★

AIR WAR

The hands of one of the several clocks on the wall were showing about 2:30 in the morning. Although the men in CENTCOM's underground bunker couldn't see outside, they knew the sky was black and the weather clear and cold—an ideal combination. Planes perform better in cold dry air, and it is consequently harder for antiaircraft fire to hit them. The deadline in the ultimatum to Saddam Hussein had passed almost twenty-four hours earlier. His troops hadn't moved, so we were going to.

The atmosphere was tense and few officers were saying much. Just before a battle, when everything that can be done has been done, everyone becomes subdued. Battles aren't foot-

games. Players don't pump themselves up by jumping up and down and giving each other the "high-five." In battle, points scored mean people killed. Just before a battle starts, every soldier is alone with his personal thoughts.

The Old Man called for everyone to gather around so the chaplain could say a prayer. When the chaplain had finished and those present had raised their heads, someone turned on a tape recorder and the room filled with Lee Greenwood's song, "God Bless the U.S.A." It was a nice touch.

"Gentlemen, let's do our job."

Thirty minutes later in the Persian Gulf, there was a blast of fire and smoke as a rocket ignited and pushed a Tomahawk into the sky. When the cruise missile was high enough, the rocket motor flamed out and the missile began to nose over. Then its stubby wings snapped into place, its air-breathing engine started, and it headed north, toward Baghdad. Operation Desert Shield had ended. Operation Desert Storm had begun.

Elsewhere, pilots were in their cockpits, ready to be launched or cleared for takeoff. The low-flying cruise missiles would be difficult for the Iraqis to detect, but they were slower than manned jet airplanes, so they had to be given a head start. The first airplanes to go would be the F-117A Stealth fighter-bombers and the electronic countermeasure (ECM) aircraft. The

Stealth bombers could get through the Iraqi radar system without being picked up, but conventional fighter-bombers needed help.

Air Force EF-111 Ravens, F-4G Wild Weasels, and Navy EA-6B Prowlers took off first to neutralize Saddam Hussein's air defense system. All sent high-powered signals that jammed radar. Some of the jamming caused Iraqi radar screens to fill with snow instead of blips from the incoming Allied aircraft. Some sent false signals that made the Iraqi radars think the aircraft were somewhere else. Some ECM aircraft carried HARM missiles to destroy radar transmitters. The HARM, or "High-speed, Anti-Radiation (radar not nuclear) Missile," locked onto Iraqi radar transmissions, followed them to their sources, and blew up the transmitters.

As the ECM planes made safe paths through Saddam Hussein's radar-controlled air defense system, they were followed by a variety of Allied fighters. Unless Saddam Hussein could scramble his fighters in time, our own fighters would have little to do. If he did put them into the air, they would be busy because their job was to protect the fighter-bombers that actually bombed the targets on the ground.

Last off were attack aircraft carrying the bombs and guided conventional munitions (GCM). Although each service kept its own planes together in packets because they were used to working together, the skies over Kuwait and Iraq were filled with many different aircraft types.

Navy A-6E Intruders, F/A-18 Hornets, and A-7 Corsairs were catapulted from aircraft carriers in the Persian Gulf and Red Sea. Air Force and Allied F-15E Strike Eagles, F-16C Fighting Falcons, F-111 Aardvarks, and British-French Jaguars and Tornados took off from land bases in Saudi Arabia and the Gulf. Giant Air Force B-52G Stratofortresses came in from Diego Garcia and locations outside the Middle East.

Navy E-2C Hawkeyes circled over the waters of the Gulf to provide early warning, and to control the fighters flying air cap over the ships. The Navy had seen the damage done to the British by Argentine Exocets in the Falklands. During the Iran–Iraq war, an Iraqi airplane had badly wounded the USS Stark with an Exocet. The Navy wasn't going to let it happen again.

Well back were the big E-3 AWACS Sentries, with their cookie-shaped radar antennas slowly spinning above their fuselages. They were monitoring everything, both the Allies and the Iraqis. Should Saddam Hussein realize he was being attacked and scramble his fighters, the AWACS would vector friendly fighters to take care of them.

The massive and complex air attack had taken months to put together. Now General

Schwarzkopf, the man in charge of everything, could only sit and wait to see if it was going to work. This was Lieutenant General Chuck Horner's and Brigadier General Buster Glosson's show. They and the Navy had planned it. They were controlling it. For the time being, Norm Schwarzkopf was a spectator.

★

It was three hours before dawn in Baghdad, but only late afternoon in the United States. That was a lousy difference of time for television reporters in the Middle East. They had to spend all day tracking down bits of information. Then in the evening they had to put together something to report on live television. Their bosses in the States wanted to start broadcasting around 5 P.M. on the East Coast, meaning the reporters had to be on call at 3 A.M. local time. Then, they could only catch a few hours sleep before they had to repeat the cycle.

January 17 looked like it might be the day. Baghdad was ten hours ahead of New York, so it had been just over twenty-four hours after the United Nations deadline had expired. No one—except the attackers—knew when the air war would begin, but Administration officials had said it would be "sooner rather than later."

CNN's Peter Arnett, Bernard Shaw, and John

Holliman were set up in their room on the ninth floor of the Al-Rashid Hotel in Baghdad. Like the lull before any storm, very little had been happening in Baghdad since the deadline had expired. There wasn't much to talk about, so the reporters were just "winging" it: some local color, how quiet everything was, and how nothing was happening—the kind of stuff television editors and anchors hate. Then in the background viewers could hear some unidentifiable noises. Off mike, one of the reporters yelled something happening outside the window. Saddam Hussein now knew he was at war with the most powerful country in the world.

> "I have seen in your eyes a fire of determination to get this war job done quickly. My confidence in you is total. Our cause is just. Now you must be the thunder and lightning of Desert Storm."

At last the troops on the ground knew they were at war.

★

In the first days of the war the news media went wild. They were receiving daily briefings by U.S. and Allied officers in Riyadh and Washington, but that wasn't enough. Having learned

many painful lessons from Vietnam, Schwarzkopf and the Pentagon weren't going to repeat
past errors in this war. The reporters were only
going to be told facts that had been totally verified—and nothing more. No targets would be
reported destroyed unless their destruction had
been absolutely verified. A Pentagon briefer had
slipped at the very beginning and reported the
Republican Guards as being "decimated" by B-
52 strikes. That set off a storm of questions about
what he meant by the word "decimate." Was it
in the literal sense of having killed one of every
ten soldiers or tanks? Or was it meant to be
figurative? Had they been almost wiped out?
Already-cautious briefers chose their words ever
more wisely.

When reporters kept pushing for more de-
tails, the military fell back on the need to conduct "bomb damage assessment," or "BDA."
Then they had to give the reporters a lecture on
what BDA was, how it was done, and why it
sometimes gave contradictory results. That evening every network news anchor was throwing
"BDA" around as though they had been using
the expression all their lives. Then "collateral
damage" became the buzz word, particularly
when CNN started televising destroyed Iraqi
homes. It went on and on.

Many reporters who knew little or nothing
about the military began speculating, and that

speculation grew to be accepted as fact by others. Most thought the air campaign would go on for about a week or ten days before the ground offensive came. Then when there wasn't a ground attack when expected, they blamed it on having to divert aircraft to search for Scuds. There was so much erroneous information and conjecture that no one but Schwarzkopf and his senior commanders really knew what was happening—but they were the ones that counted.

Aircraft losses and friendly casualties were astoundingly low. Everyone knew that the United States had worked hard and spent billions of dollars to figure out how to defeat Soviet air defense systems. Everyone knew we had good airplanes, good equipment, and good pilots—*but this good?* In the first 2,000 sorties, only eight Allied aircraft had been lost.* This was only 10 to 12 percent of the Israeli air force's loss rate in their 1973 war, and they had been considered the best in the world. At the end of the first week, U.S. and Allied pilots had reported shooting down or destroying forty-one Iraqi aircraft. We had lost thirteen and our allies had lost six, none of them in aerial combat.

Although some news reports said otherwise, the air campaign was to be conducted in three phases: strategic, operational, and tactical. The

*A sortie is one flight by one airplane.

types of targets would be the same throughout the whole war (air and ground), but the emphasis would change in each phase.

In the strategic phase the emphasis was on things that were the most dangerous. Allied planes struck hard at Saddam Hussein's command and control system, the communications network he needed to run his army. If Saddam Hussein couldn't talk to his generals, and they couldn't talk to their soldiers, there wouldn't be an Iraqi army. There would just be groups of armed but confused men. It would never be possible to knock communications out completely, but hitting key communications sites would make Saddam Hussein's job very difficult. As the Iraqis put new sites into operation, Allied warplanes lifted off to strike them.

To be able to do its other jobs effectively, the Air Force needed to knock out as much as possible of Saddam Hussein's air force and air defense weapons. A bomber couldn't drop bombs very accurately if it had to dodge surface-to-air missiles (SAMs) or break off to fight or evade an Iraqi aircraft. This was never a number-two priority. It always tied with whatever the expressed number-one priority was at the time.

Then there were Saddam Hussein's nuclear, chemical, and biological weapons and the plants that produced them. Although various intelligence sources disagreed about how soon Saddam

Hussein would have "the bomb," everyone agreed that he would make it someday. That capability had to be destroyed, but very carefully. The target planners worked on this one quite awhile before they came up with a way to do it without releasing radiation into the atmosphere. After consulting with nuclear experts, they decided to hit the concrete building in such a way that it would collapse on top of the reactor.

Finally, there were the Scud missiles and their launchers. Some were the standard Soviet-built "erector-launcher" vehicles, but Saddam Hussein had built his own "do-it-yourself" launcher. Intelligence estimated that he had between thirty and fifty launchers.* Months before, Saddam Hussein had said that he would fire missiles at Israel the moment he was attacked. Schwarzkopf believed him, so Scud launchers were a top priority.

The operational phase would begin when almost all the dangerous targets had been destroyed. The Air Force would have to "revisit" airfields it had hit before, because the Iraqis would try to repair bomb-damaged runways. It also would have to knock out a new communications site whenever it began transmitting, but in phase two the emphasis shifted.

---

*They soon found that they had been wrong. Although the Air Force got most of the Scuds in the first couple of days, Saddam Hussein was still firing them almost to the end of the war. He probably had more than 150.

The Iraqi troops in Kuwait and southern Iraq had to be isolated. That meant bombing bridges, roads, and other lines of communication, as the military calls them. If the Air Force could keep Saddam Hussein from resupplying his troops, they wouldn't be able to last. They continually needed food, water, fuel, and other supplies. They could only eat a loaf of bread once, then they'd need another.

As many of the thousands of Republican Guard and regular army tanks and artillery pieces as possible had to be destroyed before Schwarzkopf launched a ground offensive. As the air war began, Lieutenant General Kelly told the press that Saddam Hussein had 4,200 tanks, 2,800 armored personnel carriers, 3,100 artillery guns, and 545,000 soldiers in or next to Kuwait. It was going to take time and a lot of air strikes to reduce these numbers.

The tactical phase was the last phase. Some aircraft would still be hitting previous targets, but most would be supporting the ground attack. They would be needed to help break through the "Saddam Line." Despite what some were saying about a ten-day air war, it and the tactical air phase wouldn't begin until the Allied top brass gave the order.

But before Schwarzkopf could finally approve a starting date for the ground war, he would have to weigh at least a half-dozen factors:

The aircraft and their sophisticated systems continually needed maintenance. They couldn't be flown constantly without adequate maintenance or they would start falling out of the sky. The longer the air war lasted, the fewer serviceable airplanes and fresh, experienced pilots there would be. More planes and pilots could be brought in from elsewhere, but keeping those on hand fully operational was a consideration.

A certain amount of ordnance had to be available to support the ground attack, and it had to be large. As the Air Force dropped bombs and fired missiles, the stockpile would begin to go down. Ships were en route with more ammunition, but there couldn't be a letup in the bombing or a pause between the air and ground campaigns.

The condition of the Iraqis had to be monitored constantly. The faster they were "attrited," the sooner the troops could cross the border.*

VII Corps, CENTCOM's heavy attack force, had not been in Saudi Arabia very long, and some of its equipment was still arriving. It was going to take time to get the corps ready to attack.

Weather was also a consideration. The cold northern winds in January and February pro-

---

*A month after the start of the air war, the Pentagon claimed it could only *verify* having destroyed 33 percent of the 4,200 tanks and 38 percent of the enemy's 1,200 artillery pieces.

duce frequent sand and dust storms. Visibility drops and periodic rain turns the desert to mud. It's not a good time of the year, but better than March, when the *real* sandstorms hit.

The last major consideration was political, but like the weather, General Schwarzkopf had no control over it. Anything—the Israeli situation, American public opinion, Moslem demonstrations, a terrorist act—could force President Bush to order Schwarzkopf to go before he wanted.

Despite political considerations, George Bush was letting professionals run the war. He had learned a lesson from blunders in Panama in October 1989. Initially the President hadn't given General Maxwell Thurman clear guidance or enough authority in Panama. When a group of Panamanian officers tried a coup against Manuel Noriega, Thurman couldn't get through to the President in time to get permission to help the anti-Noriega forces. The coup failed and two months later Bush had to authorize a full-scale invasion of Panama.

Fighting a war requires dedicated and brave soldiers, but they also must be well trained and smart. That was why Saddam Hussein was already losing the desert war, even though it had only begun.

★

Barely twenty-four hours after the first Tomahawk missile hit Baghdad, Schwarzkopf had his first crisis. The Iraqis had launched Scud missiles at Tel Aviv and Haifa. Most exploded harmlessly in unpopulated areas, but one injured twelve civilians. Now Norman had to worry about the Israelis retaliating. If they did, that would put strains on the Allied coalition.

Two hours later, at Dhahran, Saudi Arabia, there were two loud bangs and two spots of bright light streaking across the sky. At first almost no one knew what they were, but within days the noise and light would be recognized by everyone—American Patriot missiles on their way to intercept a Scud. It was the first time the Patriot had ever been used in combat, and the large explosion in the sky showed that it worked.

In the afternoon, Scud-hunting planes spotted eleven mobile missile launchers and destroyed at least six. Three of the Scuds had been aimed at Saudi Arabia.

On the second day, Turkey, to the surprise of some, gave permission to use its military bases to launch air attacks against Iraq. Now Saddam Hussein was catching it from both ends.

At 8 that night, the U.S. guided-missile frigate *Nicholas* raided eleven Kuwaiti oil platforms. In the firefight the Navy killed five Iraqi soldiers and captured twenty-three, the first prisoners of the war.

On Saturday, January 19, three more Iraqi Scuds hit Israel, injuring seventeen people. Immediately, Patriots and American crews to operate them were airlifted to Israel. The United States was working hard to convince the Israeli government not to retaliate.

For several days, American television viewers had been entertained with stories about all the "gee-whiz" high-technology hardware their military had. What most didn't remember is that America had first started using "smart" bombs in Vietnam. They'd forgotten the television images of North Vietnamese bridges being destroyed. Today the munitions are smarter, but we've had twenty years to make them better.

The worst television images on Sunday were the Iraqis' displaying captured Allied pilots, coupled with an announcement that they would be used as human shields. It was another stupid move by Saddam Hussein, because it only infuriated the American people. Many were surprised that one of the prisoners was an Italian. Maybe because their governments wished to keep a low profile, there hadn't been much said about the French, Canadian, and Italian pilots who were attacking Iraq.

For some Americans this would be the last time to watch television for a while. The President announced he was calling up another

200,000 reservists. Many of those men and women were going to see the war at closer range.

Despite Schwarzkopf's pilots' best efforts, the Scuds kept coming toward Saudi Arabia and Israel. The Patriots knocked most harmlessly out of the sky, but one hit Tel Aviv. Three civilians were killed and almost a hundred were wounded.

By the end of the first week, the Allies had racked up a fantastic score. They had knocked out almost all the Iraqi air bases. A few were still functioning, but there had been very few Iraqi aircraft taking to the air. Not one of Saddam Hussein's airplanes had shot down an Allied aircraft. Nineteen were lost to SAMs and ground fire (thirteen U.S. and six allied). So far, only six Americans had been killed in action. One had been wounded, and fourteen were captured or missing. General Schwarzkopf's people owned the sky.

★

Week two began with more of the same. There were more Scud attacks against Israel and Saudi Arabia. No one had been hurt in Saudi Arabia, but one civilian was killed and forty more injured in Israel. Brigadier General Neal, got a laugh at one of his briefings in Riyadh, when he remarked that Saddam Hussein had a pretty dynamic zero-defect program. Neal had just passed on a report noting that Saddam Hussein had executed the commanders of his air force and his air defense system.

On Saturday, January 26, the U.S. Marines fired 155mm howitzers at Iraqi soldiers in Kuwait. It was the first time the press was told about action by the ground troops. They were not told that Schwarzkopf already had long-range reconnaissance patrols roaming around Kuwait and southern Iraq, spotting targets, looking for Scud launchers, and finding out what they could about the Iraqis.

Being constantly bombed by the Allies wasn't helping Iraqi troop morale, but most couldn't take effective countermeasures. Shooting everything they had into the sky wasn't working. Instead of seeing enemy planes fall, they had to duck as their own antiaircraft rounds and shrapnel fell back to earth. Some Iraqi pilots decided they'd had enough and tried to fly their planes to Iran. Some made it, but others were shot down before they could get to safety.

Schwarzkopf's ground troops were dug in well south of the Kuwaiti border, mostly out of range of Iraqi artillery. Like the reporters who visited them, they were getting antsy. It was pretty clear to even the lowest-ranking private that Saddam Hussein wasn't going to give up and go back to Iraq. What they saw and heard of the air war was great, but everyone expected to attack the Saddam Line sooner or later. Meanwhile, the only real excitement was patrolling north to look for Iraqis who might have crossed the border.

At midnight on January 30, a Marine patrol was checking the deserted Saudi town of Ras Al-Khafji. Just to the north, three Iraqi battalions had crossed the border with tanks and troops in armored personnel carriers. Some of the fifty tanks and armored vehicles headed toward Khafji. According to some reports, the tanks advanced with their turrets rotated to the rear, so their main guns pointed backward in the universal sign of surrender. As the Iraqis closed on Khafji, they quickly swiveled their guns around and began firing.

This sort of development was exactly why the young Marines had been patrolling the no-man's land, but giving early warning is one thing, fighting tanks is something else. Immediately the Marines called for artillery and close air support and began returning fire with TOW antitank missiles.

Marine AH-1 Cobra helicopter gunships, A-6 Intruders, and Air Force A-10 tank-busting Thunderbolts attacked the Iraqis at Khafji and at the three other locations where they had crossed the border. Half the Iraqi tanks were knocked out, and all but the battalion occupying Khafji fled back across the border—even reinforced, there

weren't nearly enough Marines to hold a town.
After losing eleven men killed and three light
armored vehicles destroyed, most of the Marines
pulled back and left the town to the Iraqis. A few
Marines who had become separated from the
rest hid in a building, hoping someone would
come or the Iraqis would withdraw before they
were discovered.

Schwarzkopf and General Boomer knew that
several Marines were missing, but Khafji is a
Saudi town. If the U.S. 1st Marine Division went
in and retook it, it would be bad for Allied relations. The next day, with American fire support,
Saudi and Qatari forces battled their way into
the town. When the fighting was finally ended,
the town was back in Allied hands. The streets
were littered with burned-out Iraqi armored vehicles and hundreds of bodies. Several hundred
Iraqis surrendered and were taken prisoner. No
friendly Arab casualties were given, but the hid-
ing Marines were rescued safely. Unfortunately,
an investigation determined that seven of the
eleven Marines killed in the action were hit by a
U.S. Maverick missile. General Schwarzkopf was
not happy, but he understood. Orders were given
to shoot Iraqi tanks on sight, whether their main
guns were turned to the rear or not.

★

Week three began with what everyone had been talking about for months. A female American soldier and her male colleague were reported missing after their vehicle was found abandoned near the Iraqi border. The Army had been looking for them for some time, but when the vehicle was discovered, it was determined the missing soldiers had made a wrong turn somewhere in the desert. Now Americans might find out how they would react when their daughters come home in body bags.

Schwarzkopf didn't have time to worry about missing soldiers. Intelligence was reporting that at least 60,000 Iraqis were massing near Al Wafra, preparing to attack south. Air attack sorties were diverted to break up the Iraqi formation.

The battleships *Missouri* and *Wisconsin* opened up with their 16-inch guns and began firing 2,700-pound high-explosive shells into Kuwait. Everyone in CENTCOM's command bunker agreed that the shelling should get the Iraqis' attention. By Sunday, February 3, Allied air forces had flown more than 40,000 sorties. Nothing in the history of warfare compares to this air campaign—and we had lost only thirty-two aircraft (twenty-three of which were American).

Ground units were making more artillery raids across the border. The self-propelled guns raced north until they could reach well into

Kuwait. Once in position, they quickly fired volleys of high-explosive shells at the Iraqis. Before the Iraqis could locate them, they turned around and roared back out of range. If Saddam Hussein had had the Americans' ability for counter-battery fire, his forces could have hit the Allies before our guns were able to withdraw.

The following week the artillery raids got even bigger. This time, besides a Marine artillery battalion, there were three Saudi artillery and multiple-launch rocket system (MLRS) battalions, the battleship *Missouri*, and air strikes. Everyone shot at the area in Kuwait where Iraqi tanks and artillery were massed. The Iraqis were pounded for three hours, then the Allies pulled out and moved back out of range. *Forty-five minutes* later a few Iraqi artillery rounds were fired back, but the nearest landed a mile away from Allied troops. It was clear Saddam Hussein's army, though big, was not very good.

The United States Marine Corps was not happy with United States Army General H. Norman Schwarzkopf—at least the top Marine generals were not. Out in the Persian Gulf, 17,000 Marines were moving into place after having practiced amphibious landings for months. The Marines were ready to go, and the reporters were reporting everything they could about the Marines' movement. But it proved a hoax. Norm Schwarzkopf had no intention of using Marines to invade Kuwait, but that was a closely guarded secret. Unless they were *really* needed, they were not going to leave their ships. The ruse was designed to keep Iraqi infantry divisions away from where the ground attack would come.

★

Besides the massive oil slick that Saddam Hussein released into the Persian Gulf, the big event in week four was Defense Secretary Cheney's and General Colin Powell's meeting with General Schwarzkopf. The CENTCOM staff had been getting information together so Norm could brief his plans for the ground offensive. They had been feeding statistics and reports to the Pentagon constantly, so there wasn't much in the way of information that had to be specially updated. The plan of attack was pretty well fixed already.

The Scud attacks were still taking place, and Schwarzkopf was not happy about that. Every time the Air Force knocked out a launcher, another one seemed to pop up somewhere else. General Horner had aircraft patrolling all over western Iraq, but the damned things could hide almost anywhere, either in a wadi or under camouflage. Hunting Scuds was using up a lot of air sorties, but it had to be done.

It was clear, even without interrogating the thousand Iraqi prisoners of war now in Allied hands, that Iraqi morale was bad. After almost a month of bombing, most of Saddam Hussein's troops would desert if they could get through their own minefields.

Everything was going well, until Wednesday, February 13. The air tasking order for that night had included an underground command and control bunker in Baghdad, known as Amiriya. The order assigned F-117A Stealth fighters to strike the bunker with two laser-guided bombs. There was intelligence showing the bunker to be militarily active, but none showing that hundreds of Iraqi civilians had moved into it after dark.

The strike was on target, but as soon as it was daylight, the Iraqis were showing foreign journalists the dead and wounded civilians. Now everyone was catching heat over what the press was reporting as a terrible mistake. Stormin' Norman was an angry man. CENTCOM had been going out of its way to avoid hitting civilians, but it was getting damned little credit for that. The White House and the Pentagon wanted every shred of information on why the Amiriya bunker had been picked as a target. It was the biggest story since Khafji, but it was trouble. Now the Joint Chiefs of Staff wanted more say in what targets were selected.

★

On February 15, a U.S. Air Force F-15E Strike Eagle shot down an Iraqi aircraft. There were so few Iraqi aircraft flying that it would have been an event under any circumstances, but this one was really different. The F-15E had used a laser-guided *bomb* to blow a hovering Iraqi helicopter out of the sky. That story took the edge off the static generated as a result of the Amiriya bunker strike.

That same day in week five, Radio Baghdad reported that Saddam Hussein was willing to withdraw from Kuwait, but only under conditions that were unacceptable to the Allies. So the war continued.

Ground skirmishes were more frequent. On February 17 alone, there were seven firefights. Some were short, but some lasted as long as two hours. On February 19, patrols from the Army's 1st Mechanized Infantry Division and the U.S. 2d Marine Division fought separately with the Iraqis. No Americans were killed or wounded. The next day, one American soldier was killed and six wounded in another fight. The Iraqis lost five tanks and twenty artillery pieces. The ground war was heating up. In four days it would come to a boil.

10

★ ★ ★ ★

PRELUDE

In only a couple of weeks the air campaign had made tremendous progress toward accomplishing the major objectives of destroying Saddam Hussein's nuclear, chemical, and biological production capability; eliminating any threat from the Iraqi air force; and neutralizing the Iraqi military's command and control system. The Scuds were a major problem because so many aircraft had to be diverted to searching for and destroying them, but except for that things were going extremely well—almost too well. A wave of speculation swept the States that this might actually be the first war ever won without ground troops. No one wanted more Allied casualties than were absolutely necessary, and influential people all around the world were beginning to argue that there was no need to send in the infantry and tanks. Always searching for a new angle, some news reporters and columnists suggested that if a ground war did start, it would be because the Army and Marine Corps didn't want the Air Force to get all the medals and glory.

If Norm Schwarzkopf had agreed with the armchair strategists and just let the Air Force bomb Saddam Hussein into submission, he would have returned to the United States as a national hero, but he wouldn't have accomplished the mission he'd been given.

Justifying a war to the people whose sons and daughters have to fight it is probably a leader's most difficult task, but it's not unlike marketing a commercial product. President Bush emphasized the "rape of Kuwait" because he knew that would be a more effective theme than any other. He had tried the strategic importance approach, but the antiwar movement had turned that into "No blood for oil." The "vicious dictator" angle was almost a non-starter, because the world is filled with dictators just like Saddam Hussein. The United States didn't send troops to Uganda to save the people from Idi Amin, or to Cambodia to get rid of Pol Pot, or to any one of a dozen countries. (General Noriega sits in a Miami jail today only because he refused to go away quietly

Gen. Schwarzkopf holds up a bottle of sand from the beach at Kuwait City during a 12 March 1991 tour of the area.
AP/WIDE WORLD PHOTOS

Gen. Schwarzkopf escorts Iraqi Lt. Gen. Sultan Hashim Ahmed (third from left) and other Iraqi military leaders to a tent prior to the start of a 3 March 1991 meeting to set the terms for a permanent ceasefire. AP/WIDE WORLD PHOTOS

Gen. Schwarzkopf stands at attention with Saudi Arabian King Fahd, during the king's 6 January 1991 visit to review U.S. and Allied troops in eastern Saudi Arabia.

Technical Sergeant George Tallent
from South Carolina inscribes a
message on a 2000-pound bomb
attached to an
F-16 fighter plane
bound for a 25 January 1991
bombing mission over Iraq.
AP/WIDE WORLD PHOTOS

A crewman salutes an A-10
Warthog attack plane on its
arrival in Saudi Arabia,
29 December 1990.
AP/WIDE WORLD PHOTOS

A Sea King helicopter from Britain's 846 Royal Navy Air Squadron flies over a blazing oil field on the outskirts of Kuwait City, 7 March 1991. AP/WIDE WORLD PHOTOS

A U.S. Marine M-60 tank and an amphibious tracked vehicle explode land mines during a 13 February 1991 ground-warfare training exercise in the Saudi desert. AP/WIDE WORLD PHOTOS

U.S. Army 155-mm self-propelled howitzers assigned to the 7th Corps head for the Kuwaiti border on 18 January 1991. AP/WIDE WORLD PHOTOS

Listening to President Bush's 15 August 1990 Pentagon speech: (from left) Chief of Staff John Sununu, National Security Adviser Brent Scowcroft, and Gen. Schwarzkopf. AP/WIDE WORLD PHOTOS

Gen. Schwarzkopf gazes from the window of his small jet on his way to visit U.S. troops in Saudi Arabia, 13 January 1991. AP/WIDE WORLD PHOTOS

Maj. H. Norman Schwarzkopf and a Vietnamese paratrooper help a wounded paratrooper after a mortar attack by Viet Cong on Duc Co, 7 August 1965. Schwarzkopf served as senior adviser to Vietnamese paratroopers in Duc Co. AP/WIDE WORLD PHOTOS

Gen. Schwarzkopf addresses troops from the 354th Tactical Air Force Wing on 31 August 1990. REUTERS/BETTMAN

Gen. Schwarzkopf confers with Chairman of the Joint Chiefs of Staff Gen. Colin Powell during Powell's and Secretary of Defense Dick Cheney's 8 February 1991 visit to Saudi Arabia. REUTERS/BETTMAN

Visiting with members of the 2nd Marine Division near the coalition forces' front lines, 14 February 1991. AP/WIDE WORLD PHOTOS

U.S. helicopters swarm in on a fuel depot in eastern Saudi Arabia, 23 January 1991. AP/WIDE WORLD PHOTOS

An F-117 Stealth fighter at an air base in Saudi Arabia. The high-tech jets, which do not show up on radar screens, saw heavy action in the war with Iraq. AP/WIDE WORLD PHOTOS

Coalition troops heading for their final destination in Kuwait.
AP/WIDE WORLD PHOTOS

Gen. H. Norman Schwarzkopf in Saudi Arabia.
© 1991 DENNIS BRACK/BLACK STAR

The general with the troops at a Patriot missile base, 29 January 1991. © 1991 DAVID TURNLEY/ BLACK STAR/DETROIT FREE PRESS

Schwarzkopf confers with Saudi Arabian Lt. Gen. Khalid Bin Sultan, commander of multinational forces in the war theater, 19 December 1990. AP/WIDE WORLD PHOTOS

The Supreme Allied Commander accompanies Saudi King Fahd as he reviews U.S. Troops at an air base in eastern Saudi Arabia, 7 January 1991. AP/WIDE WORLD PHOTOS

The chain of command: Secretary of Defense Dick Cheney (center), Chairman of the Joint Chiefs of Staff, Gen. Colin Powell (left), and theater commander Gen. H. Norman Schwarzkopf in Riyadh, 10 February 1991. AP/WIDE WORLD PHOTOS

An unidentified civilian bodyguard for Gen. Schwarzkopf walks between the general and U.S. troops during a review of forces, 7 January 1991. AP/WIDE WORLD PHOTOS

Gen. H. Norman Schwarzkopf, Supreme Allied Commander, in Saudi Arabia. © 1991 DENNIS BRACK/BLACK STAR

and had the gall to challenge the United States openly.) Why should we expend billions of dollars and possibly tens of thousands of American lives to go after Saddam Hussein?

Nor could Bush cite the "special relationship with Kuwait." On the contrary, he really had to play that down. The United States and Kuwait had had pretty rocky relations since the 1967 Israeli–Arab War. Few Arab countries had been more critical of the United States than Kuwait. For almost twenty years the Kuwaiti press blasted the United States and blamed the Americans for just about everything that was bad in the Middle East. Then the Iran–Iraq war came along and scared the hell out of the Kuwaitis. First they asked to buy some American F-16 fighters and Stinger anti-aircraft missiles. When Washington said no, they started dealing with the Soviet Union, forcing President Reagan to change his mind. Then in 1987, when oil tankers in the Persian Gulf became targets in the Iran–Iraq conflict, the Kuwaitis asked the United States to protect their ships. When Reagan balked, they again went to Moscow. A short time later, Kuwaiti ship captains hauled down their flags and replaced them with the Stars and Stripes.

Somewhat surprisingly, America's past troubles with Kuwait were virtually ignored by the press, particularly the television press, which relies more on visual images than substance to keep viewer attention. Since people spend many more hours watching television than reading, the nightly pictures of Iraqi cruelties were just what President Bush needed to mobilize the country.

Was he misleading the nation? No. The United States has very real and enormously vital interests in the Middle East. If the average American couldn't appreciate how critical those interests were, the President would have to use emotion to win his support. After all we *would* stop the "rape of Kuwait" and we *would* liberate the country, but more important to our national interests, we also would neutralize Saddam Hussein and the major threat he posed in the region. Thus, General Schwarzkopf's mission wasn't to drive the Iraqi army out of Kuwait—*it was to hold it in place and destroy it.*

As shown on Map 2, the Iraqi positions in the Kuwaiti Theater of Operations (KTO) were pretty well fixed. The "Saddam Line" extended like a fishhook from just west of where the three countries come together, along the southern edge of Kuwait, and up the coast to Kuwait City. Manning this line of fortified positions, minefields, tank obstacles, and barbed wire were the lowest-quality Iraqi troops. Behind the Saddam Line, the Iraqis had positioned mobile reinforcements and tank units. When the Allies launched their ground offensive, these units could be

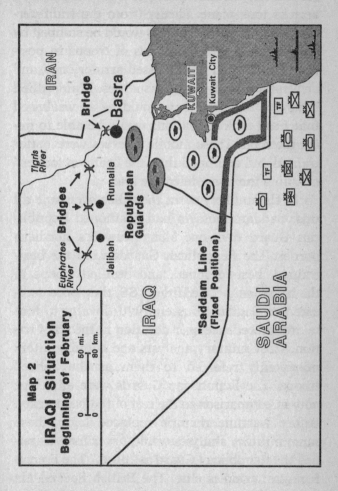

Map 2
IRAQI Situation
Beginning of February

0   50 mi.
0   80 km.

IRAN

Bridge

Basra

Tigris River

Euphrates Bridges River

Rumaila

Jalibah

Republican Guards

IRAQ

KUWAIT

Kuwait City

"Saddam Line"
(Fixed Positions)

SAUDI ARABIA

moved to wherever the main and supporting attacks took place. Ideally (from the Iraqi perspective), the Allied attacks would be stopped by the obstacles and thousands of troops in position, bombarded with massed artillery fire, and driven back with heavy casualties. If any Allied units got through, they would be so weakened that Iraqi tank formations would be able to finish them off. These mobile reserves were better trained and equipped than the "cannon fodder" manning the main defensive line.

In the unlikely event the Allies overcame all this, Saddam Hussein had positioned Republican Guard divisions along Kuwait's northern border. The Republican Guards were the best-trained, best-equipped, and best-led troops in the Iraqi army. Like Hitler's SS, they were dedicated to Saddam Hussein, with loyalty to him taking precedence over devotion to the Iraqi nation. Most military analysts and commentators mistakenly referred to them as the "elite" troops. The Republican Guards were elite, but only in comparison to the rest of the Iraqi army. Before wartime rhetoric replaced logic, these same military analysts would never have classified the Republican Guard as "elite." The French Foreign Legion is elite. The British Special Air Service (SAS) is elite. American Rangers are elite. But Saddam Hussein's Republican Guards were never as good as the average U.S. infantry unit. This is not an after-the-fact, "Gee, I guess we were wrong," statement. It has been true all along. If anyone doubts that, they should go back and read all the studies and assessments that have been done on the various armies of the world. The Iraqi army has never been classified as much above mediocre, and the word "elite" is conspicuously absent from any description of the Republican Guard.

Still, as any combat soldier knows, even a broken-down old man can kill you if he's got a gun. We do not yet know exactly how many Republican Guards there were south of the Euphrates River, but it appears to have been as many as 100,000 men, organized in three tank and three mechanized infantry divisions. That is a lot of troops and a lot of top-of-the-line guns and tanks.

Since the Republican Guard was the key to Saddam Hussein's power, the destruction of those divisions was General Schwarzkopf's primary objective. As the U.S. military says, strike the center of gravity and everything else falls. The main elements of Schwarzkopf's strategy were actually quite simple:

• Bomb the Republican Guard units and force them to dig in. The more they were bombed, the deeper they'd dig, until they were finally immobile. Air strikes alone wouldn't kill them all, but would fix the Republican Guards in position and prevent them from withdrawing north.

• Destroy the bridges across the Euphrates and Tigris rivers. This would prevent Baghdad from sending supplies of fuel, food, and ammunition to the Iraqi troops in the KTO. Equally important, it would cut off the Republican Guards. Had the liberation of Kuwait been the primary goal, the resupply routes could have been interdicted *north* of the rivers, leaving the bridges intact to encourage an Iraqi withdrawal. (Even the Pentagon agreed that the Iraqis had large amounts of ammunition, food, and supplies stockpiled inside Kuwait—probably more than needed for as long as the war was expected to last.)

• Destroy as much of the Iraqi artillery as possible before launching the ground attack. Artillery kills more soldiers than any other weapon on the battlefield. Thousand-pound bombs are impressive, but when a plane has dropped its limited load, it has to go back to base and rearm. Artillery howitzers, guns, and multiple-rocket launchers (MLRS) can rain tons of explosives on a target, and keep that rain coming almost indefinitely. Like the Soviet Red Army, Iraqis rely heavily on artillery, both in offense and defense. General Schwarzkopf had to destroy as many of Iraq's 3,100 artillery pieces as he could before any ground attack was launched.

• Do everything possible to keep from having to fight inside Kuwait City. MOBA—Military Operations in Built-up Areas—is one of the worst forms of warfare. House-to-house fighting always favors the defender, and the attacker is forced to sacrifice the advantages of speed, mobility, and firepower. Fighting for a friendly city is particularly terrible, especially when it's filled with civilians, as Kuwait City was. Everyone remembers the American officer in Vietnam saying, "We had to destroy the village to save it." Schwarzkopf wanted nothing like that to happen during Desert Storm.

Since he didn't want to have to root out the Iraqis and didn't want to hurt innocent Kuwaiti civilians, he had to demoralize the defenders and scare them into withdrawing from the city. He'd feign a Marine amphibious assault, bomb close to the town, and take his time pushing ground troops up from the south. He also would ensure there was a gap between Kuwait Bay and the Allied units coming in from the south and west so the Iraqis had a way out. Once they were clear of the city, the Allies could destroy them. In essence, this was exactly the opposite of what he intended to do with the Republican Guards.

• Finally, Schwarzkopf would delay the ground campaign as long as he could to minimize friendly casualties. Unless forced to, he didn't want to cross the Line of Departure until the bulk of the Iraqi tanks and artillery had been destroyed and the survivors had been thoroughly demoralized. Only then could he comfortably give the command to attack.

★

It had been a relatively quiet night, with only a little patrolling and a few minor firefights in the no man's land between the two armies. Even the lowest-ranking privates in the trenches and fighting holes knew the attackers would be coming soon, but there was nothing more they could do except wait. Working mostly at night, they had been digging fortifications, laying minefields, stringing barbed wire, building tank barriers, and stockpiling ammunition and supplies, expecting the enemy to attack at any moment. For some reason he hadn't, so during the past months they had built what they hoped would be an impregnable defensive system.

Just before dawn the whole horizon suddenly began flashing, and moments later the shells began screaming in and exploding among the positions. For the next fifty minutes, death rained down from thousands of artillery pieces and heavy mortars. Crouched in the deeply dug holes and bunkers, the defenders couldn't see the waves of fifty to a hundred planes repeatedly diving and adding their bombs to the mass of explosions, gray-black smoke, and flying debris. It was the most massive artillery barrage and air strike that any of the soldiers had ever experienced, and it seemed as though it would never stop.

After fifty minutes, the fire on the forward positions finally lessened. Some guns ceased firing the prep (preparation) and got ready to support the ground attack. Others shifted their aim to targets farther to the rear of the front line troops. Then through the smoke and dust, the survivors saw the infantry and tanks coming; the battle had begun.

Kuwait, February 1991? No, the World War II German–Soviet Battle of Kursk in July 1943. Paraphrasing Saddam Hussein, it was the father of General Schwarzkopf's Desert Storm.

Most military historians remember Kursk as the biggest tank battle in history, at least until the 1973 Israeli–Arab war. During the first nine days of Kursk, 2,700 German tanks and self-propelled assault guns fought 3,300 Soviet tanks. When it was over the Germans had been soundly defeated and driven back, not just to their starting point, but as much as a hundred miles farther west. And yet the Soviets didn't win because they had more tanks. They won because of the defensive system they had constructed. Antitank strong points surrounded by minefields and barriers slowed the attacking Germans so the Soviets could hit them with massed artillery. The German units that got through the first line of defense were counterattacked by Soviet T-34 tanks. Even if they defeated the counterattacks and poured additional units into the gap, the Germans still had a second defensive line to fight through, with even more Soviet armored reserves. Few German units got that far, but the ones that did found a third belt of fortifications and minefields. During nine days of fighting, the Red Army killed or wounded almost 100,000 German soldiers—and then the Soviets launched a counteroffensive. During the next five weeks the Germans attempted to break contact, but the Soviets maintained the pressure. By the time the Red Army finally outran its supply lines and had to halt, it had inflicted another 200,000 casualties on the Germans.

Unlike the battles of Moscow and Stalingrad, the Red Army had time (three months) to get ready for a major German attack, and it prepared the battlefield well. Besides killing tens of thousands of Germans, Kursk killed any chance that Hitler could win the war.

There is truth in the statement that generals spend too much of their time preparing to refight the last war. The Battle of Kursk was such a success that modern Soviet defensive doctrine is based almost entirely on that one battle. The only real changes the Soviets have made have been to adjust the battlefield for newer and more lethal weapons. But the Kursk-type defense is really not much different from that used in World War I. As shown in figures 1 and 2, the system consists of a series of fortified belts, containing company- and battalion-size strongpoints. Each belt is protected by minefields, barbed wire, and tank obstacles. Between the belts are strips of open area. Here the Soviets position reserves to reinforce where necessary, and tank units to counterattack the enemy if he makes it through the belt.

If the attacker is successful in getting through the first belt and defeats the armored counterattack, he has to repeat the process with the second belt, and then the third. Massive numbers of artillery pieces are positioned throughout the system to take the enemy under fire far beyond the forward edge of the battle area, and keep pounding him as he moves through the belts.

Saddam Hussein's Soviet advisers showed him how to fight off the enemy when the Iran–Iraq war turned sour, and it saved him from almost certain defeat. Like the Soviets, Saddam Hussein was unwilling to fool with success. When he found himself confronted by an ever-growing coalition of U.S. and allied forces, he ordered his army to dig in and build an echeloned defensive system.

The Soviet defensive system is almost im-

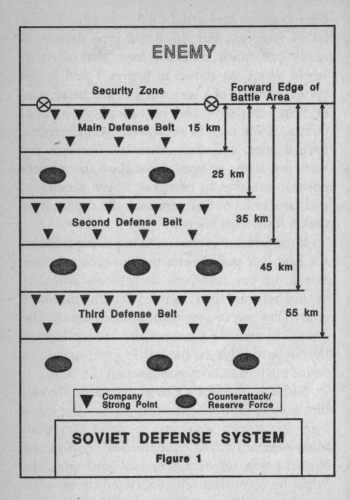

SOVIET DEFENSE SYSTEM

Figure 1

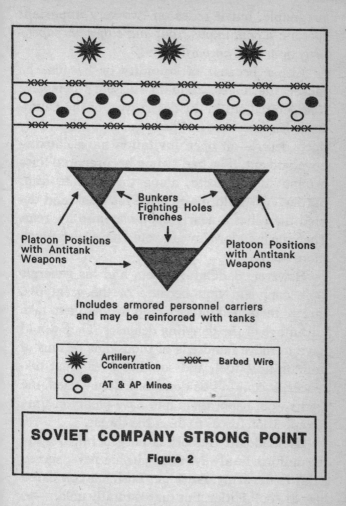

SOVIET COMPANY STRONG POINT

Figure 2

pregnable, but it relies on two very important factors: *a continuous front and either air superiority or at least air parity.*

Either because of stupidity or because he lacked the forces, Saddam Hussein's defensive line petered out in the desert west of the Saudi-Iraqi-Kuwaiti border. There was no anchor, only open desert—an open invitation for a flanking envelopment. If he had swung his prepared lines around to the north, along the Kuwaiti-Iraqi border, he would have closed his flank and denied the Allies a nearly open way into his rear. Then the fight for Kuwait would have been much more costly.

However, Saddam Hussein and his generals were confident that because of the great distances, the Allied forces would be unable to take advantage of the dangling defenses. They would have to move hundreds of thousands of tons of ammunition, fuel, and supplies over great distances. It couldn't be done, but if they tried, the Iraqis would spot them and have plenty of time to reposition forces to meet the threat.

But Saddam Hussein is no general. Despite the uniform he always wears, he has never served a day in the army. President Bush has compared him to Adolf Hitler, but that is totally unfair—to Hitler. At least Hitler had been a corporal in World War I. Saddam Hussein is merely a sadistic dictator given to executing generals who disagree with him or try to give unwanted advice. Saddam Hussein figured he could just refight the Iran–Iraq war until casualties forced the Allies to quit.

But there were a couple of problems with this line of reasoning: The Allied air campaign and General Norm Schwarzkopf. The Allies had completely eliminated Saddam Hussein's air force and were pounding his troops in Kuwait and southern Iraq. Unless Mikhail Gorbachev broke with George Bush and secretly passed Soviet satellite photos to the Iraqis, Saddam Hussein had absolutely no idea what was happening across the border.* With the massive disruption of the Iraqi communications system and tight Allied security, whatever spies Saddam Hussein had in Saudi Arabia were unable to gather and pass useful intelligence to Baghdad.

When Lieutenant General Tom Kelly used the term "battlefield preparation" in his Pentagon briefings, he completely understated the scope of the damage being done. In the first phases of the air campaign the emphasis had been on strategic targets: air defenses; command and control; nuclear, biological and chemical factories and

---

*At the time of the writing of this book there is no evidence that the Soviet Union provided any substantive intelligence to Baghdad. Although Gorbachev didn't like the idea of the Soviet-equipped and trained Iraqi army being destroyed in battle, he needed Western goodwill and Western economic and financial support far more than he needed Saddam Hussein.

stockpiles; missile sites; and so on. In mid-February the focus changed to battlefield preparation.

Back in July 1944, the U.S. VII Corps had been able to break out of the Normandy hedgerows after the Allied air forces dropped 4,200 tons of bombs on a 4.75 square mile area of the German lines. It was known as Operation Cobra and the Allies called the new technique "carpet bombing." Although General Kelly refused to use the term, that was very much what was being done to the Iraqi defenses. Forty-six years after the Normandy invasion, that same VII Corps would hit a new enemy after he, too, had been heavily bombed.

Finally, unlike Saddam Hussein and some others, General Schwarzkopf was a general—a *real* general. He, too, had studied history and Soviet doctrine, but he wasn't looking to repeat the mistakes of others. His training, experience, and near-genius IQ told him that really successful generals do the unexpected and the "impossible." His determination and famous temper convinced subordinates (and sometimes superiors) to see things his way. General Schwarzkopf told Washington and his senior officers that he was going to flank Iraq's much-touted "Saddam Line."

The idea of an attack around the Iraqis' exposed flank was not the slightest bit novel. Every infantry second lieutenant is taught to "fire and maneuver." If the forty-man platoon can handle the enemy force it has encountered, the platoon leader uses one or more of his ten-man squads to "fix" the enemy, and then he takes the rest of the platoon around to hit the bad guys on their flank. If his unit isn't large enough, his company commander attempts the same thing, using platoons instead of squads. If the company can't do it, the next higher command—the battalion—tries with companies. *Everyone* knows that the very last thing you want to do is attack an enemy position head on.

All the retired and former military officers the television networks hired to comment on the war said Norman Schwarzkopf would try to flank the Saddam Line. Naturally, they said, he would also employ secondary or "holding" attacks to fix in place as many of the Iraqi defenders as possible. Knowing that the U.S. Marine Corps would *demand* to be allowed to mount an amphibious assault on the Kuwaiti coast, many included it in their "this is what Stormin' Norman will probably do" reports. Every news magazine and paper had colorful maps showing arrows going in several directions, but always with the main one curving around to the left. It was a given—Allied ground forces would make their main attack a flanking envelopment.

The whole scheme of maneuver was so obvious that soon the analysts had to search for other things to talk about. Every characteristic of every U.S. weapons system was analyzed and explained. Citing their obligation to inform the American people and the need for a free press, the news media hired the best military talent they could find to advise Saddam Hussein on U.S. military strategy, tactics, and weapons. By merely turning on his television, any officer in the Iraqi army could get a crash course on United States military operations, taught by satellite from New York. In CENTCOM's underground command center in Riyadh, General Schwarzkopf and his staff angrily gritted their teeth and tried to ignore it.

If everyone knew that Schwarzkopf was going to make an end run, how could he really surprise the Iraqis? The answer was simply to go farther west than expected, and do it faster than anyone thought possible.

During an attack, a single mechanized infantry division needs about 3,000 tons of supplies *per day*, and an armored division needs even more. VII Corps and its divisions probably would need close to a *quarter of a million tons* of supplies for just a ten-day operation. The XVIII Airborne Corps and its units would need less, but they, too, would consume massive quantities of fuel, ammunition, and supplies. Because of the bad terrain and the almost total lack of any road network, it would take months to move 200,000 men, their vehicles and equipment, and the hundreds of thousands of tons of needed supplies beyond the end of the Saddam Line.

But General Schwarzkopf didn't have months. The longer the war dragged on, the more problems President Bush and the coalition leaders would have. It was just a matter of time before the Israelis finally got fed up and retaliated for the Iraqi Scud attacks. Americans are among the most impatient people in the world. They will support strong action provided it's short and successful. The antiwar movement never really got going, but if the war lasted too long it was bound to grow. The daily pictures from Baghdad showing dead Iraqi civilians were causing people around the world to question America's real intent. Anti-American demonstrations in Jordan and in other Moslem countries were growing larger each day. And if the Allies didn't move soon, Saddam Hussein might figure a way to escape the trap and salvage something to use later.

All these problems were discussed when General Colin Powell and Secretary of Defense Dick Cheney visited Riyadh in early February. At the end of their meeting with the Allied top brass, it was decided that the ground offensive would begin on or about February 21, less than two weeks away.

More than one month later, the CINC revealed in a television interview that 200,000 men had begun to be positioned up to 300 miles into the western desert *on January 17*! Major General William "Gus" Pagonis, commander of the 22d Theater Army Area command, was responsible for this enormous operation, which rivaled the famous World War II Red Ball Express.

11

★ ★ ★ ★

DEPLOYMENT

Virtually the whole world knew the general locations of the U.S. and Allied units. Since August, the military had taken pool reporters up to most of the units so they could get some human interest stories and catch some of the action. Some units were deployed on a line south of the Saudi border. (See Map 3.) VII and XVIII Airborne Corps units were farther south, behind the front-line divisions. Even in the desert it was pretty hard to spread out more than a dozen divisions and their supporting units, so if the military was willing, the news reporters could pick from any number of divisions to visit.

Then suddenly there didn't seem to be any trips planned to the VII and XVIII Airborne

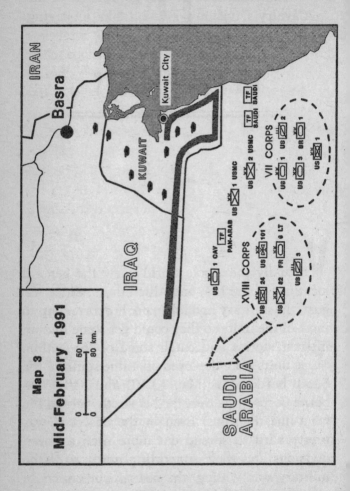

Map 3
Mid-February 1991

0   50 mi.
0   80 km.

Corps. Cameramen could still get footage of the 1st Cavalry Division's M1A1 tanks jockeying around the desert. They could still interview Marines and watch Allied artillery firing into the Iraqi lines. They were still welcome to go out in the Persian Gulf and watch the 4th Marine Expeditionary Brigade get ready for an amphibious assault. But no trips to the corps units were on the schedule. It only took a little while for the question to be asked, "What happened to VII Corps?"

After the decision had been made to launch the ground offensive on February 21, Lieutenant General John Yeosock, the commander of U.S. Army forces, ordered VII and XVIII Airborne Corps to begin secretly deploying to their attack positions far to the west. (See Map 4.)

Most people find logistics uninteresting, and war stories either ignore the subject completely or skim over it. There's little excitement in watching a thousand trucks carry supplies down a road. It's certainly not as thrilling as seeing a hundred tanks and infantry armored personnel carriers attack an enemy position. Yet when military historians thoroughly analyze Desert Storm, they will be forced to devote much space to this massive movement of hundreds of thousands of men, vehicles, helicopters, supplies, and ammunition. It would turn out to be one of the

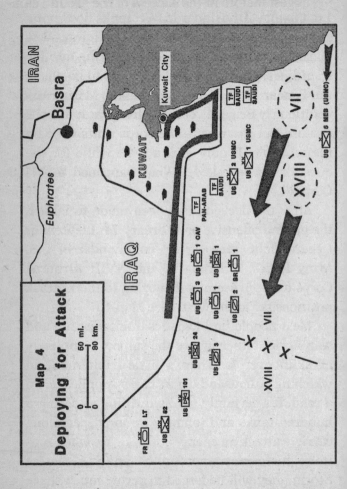

Map 4
Deploying for Attack

biggest factors in the success of the ground campaign.

Besides keeping the news media away from the moving units, Schwarzkopf stepped up his deception plan. He wanted to convince Saddam Hussein that the obvious flanking attack would come closer to the Kuwait–Iraq border, and that it would coincide with an amphibious landing on the coast.

The 1st Cavalry Division, under Brigadier General John H. Tilelli, Jr., was ordered to "demonstrate" in the Wadi al Batin, which runs along Kuwait's western border with Iraq. The military uses the word "demonstrate" to mean doing something to attract the enemy's attention, like pretending to attack. If effective, it focuses the enemy's attention on that unit and makes him move forces to react to what he thinks you are doing.

In the early days of its history, 1st Cavalry was mounted on horses. Its regiments, including George Custer's 7th Cavalry at the Little Big Horn, were the ones that fought the Indians. In Vietnam the helicopter replaced the horse and the world came to know the 1st Cav as a "glamorous" air-mobile division. After that war the Army took the helicopters away and gave the division M-1 tanks and Bradley armored fighting vehicles, making it cavalry in name only. When this powerful, heavily armed force moved, it caught people's attention. Despite the danger of losing tanks and troops to Allied air strikes, Saddam Hussein was forced to reposition some of his forces to counter this possible threat from the American cavalry division.

Meanwhile, on the right flank, the Marines and Navy continued their efforts to make the Iraqis believe that Schwarzkopf was going to launch an amphibious assault on Kuwait's coast. On February 12, in the biggest Allied-initiated ground battle thus far, the battleship USS *Missouri* began lobbing salvos of one-ton shells from its sixteen-inch guns into southern Kuwait. Added to this awesome firepower were a battalion of 1st Marine Division artillery, three battalions of Saudi artillery, and U.S. air strikes. The bombardment lasted for three hours, and was pretty convincing evidence that Schwarzkopf was serious about an amphibious landing.

Since the Iraqis had little good intelligence on Allied movements on the waters of the Persian Gulf, General Schwarzkopf made certain the news media knew that minesweepers were clearing the approaches to the Kuwaiti coast. Of course their stories were transmitted by satellite to the United States, and then to Baghdad and the world. During his briefing in Riyadh on February 27, Schwarzkopf thanked the reporters for telling Saddam Hussein exactly what he had wanted them to say. It was a sweet moment for

Norm after months of watching the media enlighten the Iraqi army on the latest American weapons and tactics.

In Baghdad Saddam Hussein saw the handwriting on the wall, but, blinded by his ego, refused to accept that he was about to lose the war. In a radio announcement Iraq stated that it would agree to pull out of Kuwait, but only under certain conditions:

• The Allies must withdraw all forces sent to the Middle East. In the translation of the Arabic text, there was some confusion about which forces Saddam Hussein actually meant—all those that arrived after August 2, or absolutely *all* forces, including U.S. naval ships that had been in and out of the Persian Gulf for years. The United States would never agree to permanently removing *all* forces.

• Israel must give up all the occupied territories—a condition the Israelis would never accept merely in exchange for Saddam Hussein's withdrawal from Kuwait.

• All United Nations resolutions against Iraq must be rescinded.

The announcement suggesting peace talks were imminent immediately brought joy to the streets of Baghdad—and, a little later, in Washington. The people of Iraq thought the war was about to end. President Bush and his coalition partners were relieved that Saddam Hussein had worded his proposal so strongly that they could reject it out of hand. The war had to end with the destruction of Saddam Hussein's military machine.

The war in the air accelerated. Every three hours, almost like clockwork, formations of giant Boeing B-52 Stratofortresses dropped tons of high explosives on Iraqi positions. Anyone who has ever been within two miles of a B-52 strike comes away with a new appreciation of what the word "awesome" really means.* (Those in the target area just *blow* apart.)

While the bombing of strategic targets and the Scud-hunting continued, the emphasis was changing to battlefield preparation. More and more Allied aircraft were being given targets or target areas to hit within Kuwait. On February 16, U.S. attack helicopters conducted their first night attack across the border. Unfortunately, the next day an AH-64 Apache fired a Hellfire guided missile and hit a U.S. armored personnel carrier (APC), killing two soldiers and wounding six. The Americans had been in close contact with an Iraqi unit, and in the predawn darkness the helicopter pilot mistook the APC for an Iraqi vehicle.

---

*Almost everything the news media say about the B-52 is true, except for one thing: Its nickname, "BUFF," does not stand for "Big Ugly Fat *Fellow*." The final "F" stands for a much more crude and graphic word.

Map 5
Theater of Operations

0   100 mi.
0   160 km.

All across the front, mortars, artillery, and aircraft attacked Iraqi patrols that were being sent out to try to find out what Schwarzkopf's troops were doing. Besides the "friendly fire" incident, there were six other clashes between Allied and Iraqi troops that same night. Two nights later, the 2d Marine Division hit an Iraqi observation post with 4.2-inch mortars and TOW antitank missiles. Elsewhere a patrol from the 1st Infantry Division tracked an Iraqi reconnaissance patrol for about four hours, before it opened up on them with machine guns. The Iraqis scurried back to the north without having learned anything.

On February 20, Allied reconnaissance spotted a concentration of 300 Iraqi tanks and vehicles about sixty miles north of the Saudi border. For the rest of the day, U.S. Air Force A-10 "Warthogs" and other aircraft repeatedly attacked them. True to form, Lieutenant General Kelly told reporters in the Pentagon that they had only *confirmed* killing twenty-eight tanks and twenty-six other vehicles. The reporters nodded seriously and scribbled away in their notebooks, oblivious to the significance of the action. An Iraqi armored or mechanized infantry division is organized into three brigades. Two of the brigades in an armored division are tank, while one is mech infantry. The ratio is reversed in a mechanized infantry division, where only one is a tank brigade, and the other two are mech infantry.

An Iraqi tank brigade has about 175 tanks and armored vehicles. When the pilots went after the concentration of 300 vehicles, they were probably attacking an Iraqi armored or mechanized infantry division—one of only eleven thought to be in the Kuwaiti Theater of Operations. General Kelly must have gone back to his office and roared with laughter when none of the reporters grasped the significance of this action. After the war General Schwarzkopf said that he had ordered his people "to tell it like it is." If he *really* said that, his officers interpreted his orders to mean, "Unless you can show them scalp, don't tell them you've hurt anybody." With the air support CENTCOM had available, and the better part of a day to use it, there is no way the pilots could have knocked out only fifty-four vehicles. They must have destroyed the better part of an entire division's combat power. If so, this battle ranks right up there with the big tank battles that occurred after the ground war started. Whatever the actual destruction was, the wave of air strikes effectively eliminated a major Iraqi counterattack force.

The business of blinding the Iraqis, softening them up, and confusing them about where the main attack would come continued, but not without cost. During the three-week period end-ing February 20, the United States lost five people killed in action and twenty-eight killed in accidents and other nonhostile incidents. Nineteen more were reported as missing in action, and one was confirmed captured. Nineteen U.S. and two Allied aircraft were lost, either shot down or crashing upon landing. More than a dozen Americans were wounded or injured. These were sad losses for the soldiers' families, but compared to almost any other war, the number of fatalities was incredibly low.

While the air and ground action was drawing all the attention, Lieutenant General Yeosock's VII and XVIII Airborne Corps were working their tails off moving to the west. Major General Pagonis was doing far better than could be expected in orchestrating the operation and relocating his supply dumps, but the task was almost unmanageable. Reluctantly, Schwarzkopf agreed to ask Washington to postpone "G"-Day another two days, until February 23.* As it happened, that was a lucky chance move.

On February 21, the Soviets announced that Saddam Hussein had agreed to a new plan to stop the fighting. If the Allies agreed to a cease-

---

*"G-Day" is a new term in the lexicon. For years the military has used "D-Day" and "H-Hour" to denote the date and time of an attack. One has to wonder if "G-Day" will be retained as an official term. If so, will we then be swamped with "A" for "air," "S" for "sea," and miscellaneous other lettered days marking military action?

fire, he would begin withdrawing his troops and have them all out of Kuwait in three weeks. The United Nations would send observers to monitor both the cease-fire and withdrawal. Iraq would release Allied prisoners of war within three days after the cease-fire, and the United Nations would lift its sanctions.

Had the Allied units been moving to or across their lines of departure (LD) when the announcement was made, trying to stop them would have created mass confusion. More important, the Iraqis might have detected the deployment of Allied forces. While the politicians were considering the new proposal, Saddam Hussein could have redeployed at least some of his forces, most notably the Republican Guards. Then, if the cease-fire proposal was rejected, Schwarzkopf's troops would have had to fight a more prepared enemy.

Not wanting Saddam Hussein to save his Republican Guards and his tanks and artillery to use against his neighbors on another day, President Bush quickly rejected the plan. The Allies would give the Iraqis only one week to get out whatever men and equipment they could. Everything left in Kuwait after those seven days would have to be abandoned.

Machine gun bullets and shell fragments might bounce off a tank's armor, but its machinery is pretty delicate. Like an animal, if it's not taken care of it will quickly die. Non-armor soldiers always shake their heads when they hear a tanker complain about the many hours of maintenance he needs to do for every hour he drives his tank. After a month of no maintenance, it probably would take a week for the Iraqis just to get their tanks and armored personnel carriers out of their holes and running. President Bush's one-week condition was really a demand for Saddam Hussein to disarm most of his heavy forces in Kuwait.

When Bush stated that the Iraqis had to begin a large-scale withdrawal by noon, Washington time, on February 23, he as good as publicly announced when the Allies would attack.

Except in the jungles of Vietnam, the U.S. military has always trained to fight at night. Its doctrine is to attack and take an objective before dawn, which forces the enemy to counterattack in broad daylight. Over the past twenty years the Army has developed night-vision devices, and now tries to conduct at least one-third of its training during the hours of darkness.

Noon in Washington, is 8:00 P.M. in Saudi Arabia. Once it was dark, the Allied troops would begin moving up to the line of departure. Then the attacks—main and supporting—would begin an hour or two before dawn. If Schwarzkopf didn't attack by about eight in the evening, Washington time, his divisions probably would have to wait another twenty-four hours. To delay meant risking detection, or chancing that Saddam Hussein would do something dramatic to save his army. That risk was too great. Many of the Allied units were within range of Iraqi artillery that hadn't been destroyed, and just one battery of five or six guns could kill or wound many American or Allied soldiers. To minimize friendly casualties, General H. Norman Schwarzkopf would have to attack within hours of President Bush's deadline.

12

★ ★ ★ ★

ATTACK!

The winter weather in northern Saudi Arabia had come as a shock to most Americans, who thought the desert was always very hot and very dry. When the paratroopers of the 82d Airborne Division arrived in August, the Saudi desert was exactly what they had expected. Since then it had turned wretchedly cold at night, with periodic rains turning the desert floor to mud. The night of February 23 was no exception: cold, overcast, and scattered light rain. But unlike previous nights, the troops of the 2d Brigade were so keyed up that most of them hardly felt the cold. After more than five months of training in the desert, and five weeks of watching and listening to the air war, it was time to kick some Iraqi butt.

Old Stormin' Norman had been running them ragged since the day they'd arrived in the theater. First, they were ordered to take up positions in northern Saudi Arabia. No one really expected the 82d Airborne to stop Saddam Hussein from coming on south, but hopefully he'd think twice before he went to war with the United States. When a reporter had asked one of the young troopers about that mission, the soldier answered that they would have been little more than "speed bumps" had Saddam Hussein decided to attack into Saudi Arabia.

When the U.S. advance forces were relieved by heavier forces, the Old Man had made them train like hell on everything that anyone knew about the Iraqi army: its tanks, weapons, tactics, fortifications, minefields—*everything*. Then a few days before G-Day they had to grab everything they owned and charge a couple hundred miles into the desert. The men were tired of all the crap and just wanted to get the real war going so they could go back home.

Actually, it had already started. The Iraqis had no fortifications this far west, and the French 6th Light Armored Division had crossed the border already the previous day. (See Map 6.) Borders didn't really mean much in this area, but

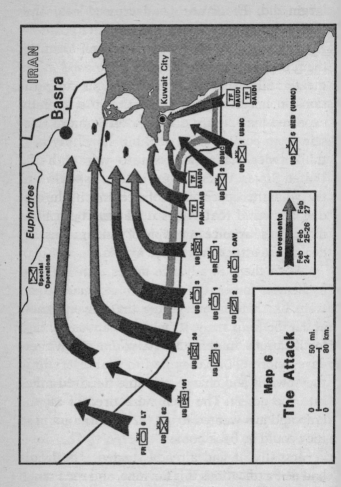

Map 6
The Attack

terrain did. The French had crossed near the Saudi town of Rafah to get into a better position for the main attack. Now, just before dawn, it was time to go the rest of the way.

The 2d Brigade had been coordinating with the French division for some time. There had been some language problem, but after more than forty years in NATO, the French, British, and Americans had gotten pretty used to each other. The French government preferred to maintain the appearance of keeping its forces independent of NATO, but it was more appearance than substance. A couple of times each year the French army participated in NATO exercises. Their government never committed itself to participate too far in advance, but it almost always did. The reserved government attitude didn't seem to carry over to the French military, because they and the other NATO forces always got along quite well.

So, while some might be surprised that the French 6th Light Division had "opcon"—operational control—over the U.S. 82d Airborne's brigade, the old NATO hands weren't. The only problem the 2d Brigade really had was trying to show the French Foreign Legionnaires that they were just as good. The Foreign Legion units had also been put under the French division commander, making the combined force one of the most distinctive units in Saudi Arabia.

The French and the 82d Airborne were on the extreme left flank of the XVIII Airborne Corps' sector. Their mission was to push quickly north toward the Iraqi airfield at As-Salman, near the Euphrates River. On the way, they were to capture a small communications center, code named "Rochambeau." Although defended by tanks and antiaircraft guns, Rochambeau was not expected to cause much of a problem for the French armor, paratroopers, and Legionnaires.

Another objective was the securing of a two-lane road that could be used to move additional troops and supplies more quickly into Iraq. Besides taking these objectives, the French and Americans were ordered to screen the XVIII Airborne Corps' flank all the way to the Euphrates. The Corps had to make certain that no Iraqi units unexpectedly came in from the west to hit them in the side or rear.

The French tanks' engines growled as the attack got underway, but the noise was not enough to drown out the sound of the artillery. Shells from French and American howitzers split the air, making an odd sound as they passed overhead: not swooshing, not exactly screeching or howling, probably more like the sound made by one of the new ultra-high-speed trains the French had told them about. In the distance they could hear the "ka-ruump" sounds as the 105mm and 155mm rounds hit the ground and exploded. They could hear more artillery to their east, but the Allies were attacking across a 300-mile front, so what they heard was just a small fraction of thousands of guns firing.

The technique being used by all the Allied forces was simple, but effective and smart. It was something the U.S. Army had practiced in Vietnam, and a tactic that Schwarzkopf and his subordinate commanders insisted upon: Use armament, *not* soldiers, to kill the enemy. Each known or suspected Iraqi position was thoroughly prepped with artillery before Allied troops moved toward it. Softening up the position, and then attacking behind a wall of artillery, provided the best chance of overrunning the enemy before he could react.

The French moved out quickly and were immediately followed by the lighter-armed paratroopers. There was little opposition as they charged north; almost all the Iraqis they ran into threw down their weapons and surrendered. By nightfall the French and Americans had driven seventy miles into Iraq and had taken a couple of thousand prisoners. It was a good first day.

★

Being the only air assault division in the theater, the 101st Airborne Division wanted to do something unique. Like the 1st Cavalry, the

101st carried a misleading name. It had been an airborne unit for most of its history, but then the Army decided that one parachute division was enough. The Army probably would have disbanded both the 101st Airborne and 1st Cavalry divisions had it not been for two things. First, both units had impressive combat records and rich heritages, and no one wanted to see those disappear. Second, many high-ranking alumni from both divisions argued to keep the units alive. So the 1st Cavalry was converted to armor and the 101st was made into air assault, but the names of both stayed the same. (The 101st Airborne carries the words "Air Assault" in parentheses after its name.)

General Schwarzkopf thoroughly angered the Marines when he told them they wouldn't be hitting the beaches, and disappointed the 82d Airborne as well by vetoing a massed parachute jump. But he and General Yeosock made the 101st Airborne happy by approving their plans to conduct the largest helicopter assault in history.

Early in the morning of G-Day, helicopters airlifted more than 2,000 of the 101st Division's troops over fifty miles into Iraq. Over the next few hours, a constant stream of choppers brought more troops and slung loads of artillery, ammunition, and light vehicles into the objective. Weather delayed part of the operation, but by midday an operating base had been established and was growing larger.

In searching for words to describe it, the Pentagon mentioned the acronym "FARP," which set reporters to laughing and trying to figure different ways to use the word. "FARP" stands for "Forward Arming and Refueling Point," sort of a quick-service gas station for helicopters. What caused the giggling at the Pentagon briefing was far more than a FARP. Forward Base Cobra, as it had been named, was twenty miles in diameter! It would be a major base to stage further operations deep into Iraq to cut the main highway between Basra and Baghdad.

Besides the sky full of choppers, a 700-truck convoy began to move men, equipment, and supplies from Saudi Arabia to Cobra. By the end of the day, the 101st Airborne had most of the division inside Iraq, with one of its brigades headed toward Objective Eagle, northwest of Nasiriya on the Euphrates River. Except for one UH-60A Black Hawk that was hit but still flyable, the division had not lost a helicopter.

★

The 24th Mechanized Infantry Division had embarked from the States by ship with only two brigades. In an effort to have as many divisions as possible with the manpower Congress had authorized, the Army had deactivated some of its brigades and replaced them with National Guard units. In theory, any war other than one with the Soviet Union could be handled by active duty units. If the Soviet leadership ever made a decision to attack Western Europe, the Warsaw Pact would have to do certain things to prepare. The United States was confident that its intelligence systems would give enough warning of an attack to allow it to get prepared. The President would activate the reserve brigades, and after a month or so of training they would join their active duty divisions.

Unfortunately, when tested the theory didn't work. Saddam Hussein's unexpected attack on Kuwait was so big that the United States couldn't handle it without stripping Europe of too many of its divisions. Then top brass discovered that it was unreasonable to expect that reserve infantry and armor units could be thrown into combat with only a month of additional training. They were willing, but the Army didn't want to risk having them slaughtered, so other active duty units were attached to the divisions. In the case of the 24th Mechanized Infantry Division, it was 197th Mechanized Infantry Brigade from Fort Benning, Georgia.

The 24th Mech Division had moved to a position west of the Saudi town of Hafar al Batin, and had deployed in preparation for G-Day. As soon as it arrived it began sending small units across the border to locate the Iraqis. Like the other Allied units, it was getting intelligence from reconnaissance aircraft and satellites, but in this business you can never get enough information. Besides, the patrols were necessary to keep the Iraqis from discovering that the Allies had shifted their forces to the west.

On February 23, the day before the ground offensive, the division ordered the 197th Brigade to send a large combat/reconnaissance patrol north to see what it could find. In this virtually undefended area west of the Saddam Line, the patrol drove almost twenty miles without finding any Iraqis. The desert was so empty that a part of the patrol remained out there so it could scout ahead of the rest of the brigade when it attacked the next day.

The offensive was to be a giant wheeling movement to the north and then swinging around to the east. That meant letting the French 6th Armored and 82d Airborne troops get a head start. Once they were rolling, the 24th Mech and the 197th Brigade could start.

The same weather that had disrupted the 101st Division's air assault operation swept over the two mechanized units. As high winds kicked up a driving sandstorm, bulldozers knocked holes in the undefended double sand berms, and the tanks and tracks (armored personnel carriers) roared north.

Near the 24th Mech, the 3d Armored Cavalry Regiment (ACR) also moved through the berms and raced forward to screen in front of corps. More lightly armed and faster units are normally given screening missions. Their job is not so much to battle the enemy, as it is to find out where he is. They will fight but are not supposed to become "decisively" engaged—a term that generally means someone loses the battle. They are only supposed to delay the enemy or hold him until a larger force can get forward and take over. Armored cavalry regiments like the 3d ACR are organized and trained for just this type mission. They are the modern-day version of the old horse cavalry.

By the end of Day One, most of the XVIII Airborne Corps, under Lieutenant General Gary Luck, was well into Iraq. True to its commander's name, the corps was meeting little opposition and taking large numbers of Iraqi prisoners. General Schwarzkopf hadn't expected much problem this far west, but things were going far better than had been expected, particularly given the size and complexity of the daring air assault.

★

In the center of CENTCOM's offensive, Lieutenant General Frederick Franks' "missing" VII Corps was on the move.* In the dark hours of night, the engineers began clearing the minefields and bulldozing gaps in the sand berms. The Iraqi defenses were a little thicker here, but much less formidable than those nearer the coast. As the engineers worked to clear paths, Iraqi artillery opened up and began dropping high-explosive shells around them. Everyone held their breath, worried that Saddam Hussein's gunners were loading chemical or biological rounds in the breeches of their guns. Allied troops all along the line had their gas masks handy, and many were wearing their heavy protective suits, but everyone prayed that it wouldn't be necessary. To most soldiers, nerve gas or biological agents were far more frightening than anything else the Iraqis could throw at them. But the rounds impacting around VII Corps had not yet made the distinctive muffled sound given off by shells that spray toxic gas. Before they could, the aerial freight train noise began passing overhead in the opposite direction. The radars and the other "gee whiz" gadgets had detected the Iraqi artillery and locked

*Not only had the VII Corps disappeared from the news reporters' schedule, it even momentarily dropped off the Pentagon's list. Because of a glitch, the page showing VII Corps units and commanders was missing from the telefax transmitted to Washington from Riyadh, at midnight on February 23.

on to the flight paths of the incoming rounds. Computers had instantly calculated the location of the guns, and then transmitted firing data to VII Corps' own artillery. Moments later the Iraqi gunners got a practical lesson in the theory of counter-battery fire. The engineers continued their work.

One of the first units through the gaps the engineers had made was the 2d Armored Cavalry Regiment. Like the XVIII Airborne Corps' 3d ACR, the 2d Armored Cav's mission was to get out front and screen. Once through the breach, the 2d ACR's tanks and armored fighting vehicles raced through, spread out, and began searching for Iraqis. Just as soon as the 2d Armored Cav was through, Major General Ronald Griffith's 1st Armored Division pushed through behind it. Everyone was relieved that getting through the Iraqi forward defenses was so easy. Now they were on the move and looking for a fight. However, by nightfall they had driven more than twenty miles into Iraq without finding any major Iraqi force.

★

Most people are a little confused about the differences between armored and mechanized infantry divisions. It's easy to visualize a tank battalion roaring across an open field, kicking up great clouds of dust and firing their big main guns at the enemy. Equally vivid are the scenes of infantrymen grimly slogging forward through a hail of machine gun fire with fixed bayonets. Somewhere between these extremes are the pictures of smaller, boxier armored personnel carriers with soldiers packed inside and clinging to their tops—the mechanized infantry.

Some people suppose that a division is "armored" because it only has tanks, and that a mech infantry division only has personnel carriers. Actually, there were relatively few differences between the 1st Armored Division and its neighbor, the 24th Mechanized Infantry Division. A typical armored or mech infantry division has around ten maneuver battalions of about 800 men each. The word "maneuver" is used because they move against the enemy and fight him face-to-face. The men in an armored battalion fight in tanks, while the infantrymen are carried into battle in their armored personnel carriers (some are called "armored fighting vehicles"). The carriers allow the infantry to move as quickly as the tanks, and their relatively thin armor lets the troops get closer to the enemy before they finally dismount and fight him on foot.

The only real difference between the armored and the mechanized infantry division is in the ratio of tank and infantry battalions they have.

An armored division might have six tank and four mechanized infantry battalions, while the ratio is reversed in a mech infantry division. Pride in his branch (and a more distinctive shoulder patch) makes the infantryman prefer to serve in a mech infantry division. On the other hand, the larger number of tanks in an armored division is pretty damn attractive. Tankers and "grunts" continually argue with each other, but they always fight *together*.

★

Major General Paul Funk's 3d Armored Division was equally successful in punching through the lightly held Iraqi line. Like its sister division, the 3d Armored spread out and roared north toward the Euphrates River and, likewise, found mostly scared and disheartened Iraqi soldiers who only wanted to surrender. Even without thirty-eight days of diving for cover from Allied air strikes, the approaching line of sand-colored, growling armored monsters would have taken away most of the Iraqis' fight. By midnight, the 3d Armored Division was nearly fifty miles into southern Iraq and had taken no losses.

★

The "Big Red One, the 1st Mechanized Infantry Division, crossed the border about sixty miles west of Kuwait, where Saddam had his strongest defenses in the VII Corps' sector. Major General Thomas Rhame was proud of his troops. He had expected that it would take most of the first day to get past the Iraqis' forward defenses, and planned to assault the main line early the next day. Instead, the dawn attack met almost no resistance, so his men were fresh and itching for a fight. Taking advantage of the situation, General Rhame ordered the attack to continue. After a thirty-minute artillery bombardment of the main line, armored combat earthmovers and dozer tanks rolled forward and began clearing paths through the minefields. Behind them came the 1st and 2d Brigade maneuver battalions. A little after 5:00 P.M. the division was through the main defenses and ready to push on. The surviving Iraqi defenders either surrendered or escaped to the north.

☆

The last unit under VII Corps was the pride of Britain—the British Army's 1st Armoured Division, including the famed "Desert Rats" who had last fought Rommel's Afrika Korps in World War II.

The news media and politicians made much of British and French contributions to the ground war, but their participation did not entail anything unusual. Except for the 1st Mechanized Infantry Division, they had all come to Saudi Arabia from Europe. In World War II, the 1st Mech (then just plain infantry) and the 3d Armor Divisions had fought under VII Corps from northern France to the German border. While VII Corps was racing through France and Belgium, the British 1st Armoured was just to the north. The U.S. 1st Armored Division had fought in Italy, but went to work for the VII Corps after the war. The Brits and the Yanks often make snide remarks about each other's marching or language, but, like the tankers and grunts, they make a hell of a team when facing a common enemy.

★

To the east, there was a very frustrated division. For days the 1st Cavalry had been playing games with the Iraqis in Wadi al Batin. The division had been ordered not to become decisively engaged, so all it had been doing was skirmishing with Iraqi troops. Both Generals Schwarzkopf and Tilelli believed that one of Saddam Hussein's biggest concentrations of troops was just to the 1st Cav's north. Now it was time to feign a major attack to draw the Iraqis in. However, in pushing miles north the Cav met with only light resistance. The brass, after considering the situation, gave the order to pull back, swing around, and come back into Iraq where the 1st Mech Division had punched through. Intelligence had picked up the movement of a Republican Guard tank division, and this redeployment was the best way to hit the Iraqis. Still, when night fell the 1st Cav had yet to do any real fighting.

★

The Marines and the Arab forces had the least glamorous and potentially most dangerous missions. They were to punch directly into the strongest part of the Saddam Line.

One of the biggest problems of coalition fighting is something the military calls "interoperability," the degree to which procedures, tactics, and weapons are the same among Allied forces. NATO forces have been struggling with interoperability for decades but still haven't solved all the problems. The U.S. Army and Marine Corps have had difficulties in the past, but they were absolutely nothing compared to the U.S.–Arab problem.

The Syrians were organized, trained, and armed much more like the Iraqis than like their coalition partners. The Egyptians were in a state of transition from all Soviet weapons and doctrine to more Western equipment and methods.

A few Egyptian and American units had previously done some joint training, but not much. Schwarzkopf had sent U.S. Special Forces teams to all the Arab units to give them a quick course on how the American Army fights. The teams were still with the Arabs to advise and coordinate with adjacent American units, but the actual battle could be tricky. U.S. Air Force air control teams, called "air commandos," were also sent—among other things, to make certain the Soviet-made T-62 being bombed was actually Iraqi and not one belonging to an ally.

Operationally, it would have been easier to put all American (and European) forces on one flank of the battlefield, and all the Arabs on the other, but political and military considerations argued against that. For political reasons, Arab forces *had* to take Kuwait City and most of the few other towns in the country. That meant deploying them on the right flank. However, they needed U.S. combat support to help them. So Schwarzkopf decided to plug in the 1st and 2d Marine Divisions, and a brigade that had been sent to Saudi Arabia from the 2d Armored Division in the States. The Americans could help punch through the Saddam Line and then provide further support where necessary.

The three Egyptian and Syrian armored and mechanized infantry divisions jumped off at dawn from just south of the Iraq–Kuwait border.

It was from there to the coast that the Allied air forces had made their heaviest effort. For days, B-52s and lighter attack aircraft had been pounding the Iraqis' forward positions. As shown in Figure 1, the Saddam Line was formidable. Before the Marines and Arabs could even get to the first line of defenses, they had to get through a minefield that was more than a mile deep. Then there were trenches, sand berms, barbed wire, barrels of napalm—all covered by Iraqi artillery and multiple-launch rocket systems (MLRS). It would have been a real bitch had it not been for the "carpet bombing" that General Kelly said he knew nothing about. It had destroyed much of the Iraqis' artillery, obstacles, and fortifications, and killed many of their soldiers. The ones that were left were shell-shocked and demoralized, graphic examples of what the term "cannon fodder" really means. Like the Americans farther to the west, the Pan-Arab task force had comparatively little problem—except with large numbers of Iraqis trying to give themselves up—and continued north.

★

The Americans had given a name to the two bends in the Kuwaiti–Saudi border. About fifty miles inland from the coast the border bends north, and that area was referred to as the "elbow." The bend where the border turns back to the west was called the "armpit." The 2d Marine Division got the armpit, and it also got the Army's 1st Brigade, 2d Armored Division, which had given itself the name the "Tiger Brigade."

Besides armored Bradley fighting vehicles, the Tiger Brigade had the latest M1 Abrams main battle tank, which was superior to the older Marine M60A3 tanks. But what was much more important was that it gave the 2d Marine Division considerably more main battle tanks than it normally had. (The two Marine divisions were infantry, not mechanized infantry. Instead of having four tank battalions, a Marine division only has one regular tank battalion and one light tank battalion.)

At 5:30 A.M. the Marines started their attack. It wasn't like landing on the beach and charging inland, and it wasn't like storming an enemy objective. It was slowly moving in six columns on the paths that had been cleared through the minefield. There was sporadic Iraqi artillery, tank, and automatic weapons fire, but nothing that slowed them down.

Shortly before noon, the Marines and the Tiger Brigade got through the Saddam Line, regrouped, and then pushed northeast. They were slowed several times by the soft sand, but made it twenty miles into Kuwait on the first day. The television news crews that accompanied the Marines ended up filming Iraqi equipment rather than the heavy fighting they expected.

★

The 1st Marine Division, which like the Army had learned a lot from Vietnam, attacked across the "elbow." As they completed crossing the minefield, the Marines' M60 tanks started taking fire from dug-in Iraqi T-55 and T-62 tanks. As they returned the fire, orbiting Air Force jets peeled off and began dropping bombs on the enemy. That convinced the surviving Iraqis that it was foolish to resist. By the end of the day, the 1st Marine Division had taken several thousand POWs.

The forces nearest the coast—the Saudis, Kuwaitis, and other forces from the Arab Gulf States—had similar experiences. Penetrating the much-talked-about Saddam Line was primarily a matter of clearing paths through the minefield, bulldozing gaps in the sand berms, and (literally) driving into Kuwait.

★

While everyone was watching the ground attack, the Allied air forces continued with their missions: strategic bombing in central and northern Iraq, Scud hunting, attacking bridges over the Tigris and Euphrates rivers, and supporting the ground assault.

Also on the ground, but completely unnoticed, were small special operations teams who had been inserted days and weeks before. When a crisis is developing somewhere in the world, news reporters who *really* know the military, know what units to keep an eye on. Any unusual activity by the truly elite units signals that something big may be about to happen. The Army's three Ranger battalions and Special Forces Detachment Delta and the Navy's SEALS ("Sea-Land-Air") are some of those units.

Of course the military knows that reporters and foreign agents watch these units, so they go to great lengths to conceal any unusual activity. Still, little things like sudden cancellations of dinner invitations tell the local military community that something is going down somewhere. Some of these special operations people disappeared from their homes several months before Desert Storm, and never surfaced in Saudi Arabia. Given the kind of mission special operations units train for, old military hands *knew* they were in Kuwait and Iraq. They just didn't know exactly where or exactly what they were doing. As General Schwarzkopf said later in his briefing, special operations teams had been behind the lines, but he wasn't going to say more. We may never know what every team did.

★

Back at the CENTCOM underground bunker in Riyadh the atmosphere was business-like, but radiating joy. (Generals are never supposed to laugh and colonels are only allowed modest chuckles.) In the biggest, most complex operation since Korea, the Allied force had captured about 15,000 Iraqis, destroyed hundreds of tanks and guns, driven well into enemy territory—and lost almost no people.

Like any old soldier, General Schwarzkopf must have been uncomfortable sitting in his underground command post, while everyone from the corps commanders down was out in the field. But like Eisenhower on D-Day, his responsibilities forced him to stay where he could run the whole operation—like Eisenhower, he was personally responsible for *everything*. So far, what he was responsible for could not have been going better.

D PLUS ONE

In working out the operations order for a big battle, planners break the phases into neat parts: "Upon taking Objective Bravo . . ." or "On D plus one . . ." However, combat never quite seems to fit neatly into discrete chunks. On the battlefield everything just flows together, particularly for the people fighting it.

At the underground bunker in Riyadh, the CENTCOM J-3 Operations officers were posting the information they were receiving from the field. The black and red marks on the large wall maps had been constantly changing since the first days of August. As friendly units moved around, situation reports (sitreps) were passed up the chain of command, using secure (scrambled) radio communications. Then the information was posted on maps and charts around the room. As Schwarzkopf's headquarters received intelligence reports from satellites, Airborne Warning and Control System (AWACS) aircraft and the mass of other intelligence sources were also brought up to date. Then there were the air ops (operations) maps for posting air and Cruise missile strikes that were still hitting all over Iraq. Off to the side were charts giving the status of critical items, such as ammunition expended and balances remaining.

Commanders at every level had the same acetate- or Plexiglass-covered maps and charts. Even the captains and lieutenants pushing through the desert sand had important information scribbled on the backs of their maps. In peacetime, makers of typing paper make big profits from their sales to the military, but in war it's the grease pencil and acetate manufacturers who get rich.

At lower levels, the maps covered smaller areas and showed more terrain features, although that was much less significant in the desert than it would have been in other areas. The information posted and the things monitored were much more detailed than in Riyadh. However, there was one chart that everyone maintained—the chart that showed the casualties. Norm Schwarzkopf wasn't entirely truthful when he said he wasn't going to get in the body-count business. He and everyone else was definitely keeping count of the important bodies—the Allies' own casualties. The prayer the chaplain had said minutes before the first Cruise missile was launched in January, must have been a good one. The Allies weren't taking just minimal casualties—*they were taking almost none at all*. Thirty-eight days of continual bombing had taken the fight out of the Iraqi army. The Air Force certainly had done its part in the new AirLand Battle doctrine.* By the end of the first day, the Army had, as well. All the hard work, late-night hours, arguing, and joint exercising

*The military insisted on spelling AirLand as one word, not because it was more catchy, but to emphasize the integration of air and land forces in the new doctrine. The services were still grappling with Navy differences, so they stayed with hyphenating the term "Air-Land-Sea." (Of course, each component started with a capital letter.)

was paying off. The first real test of the new doctrine showed that it was a winner.

Because of the attack's tremendous initial success, Norm Schwarzkopf could lean back in his oversized black leather chair and take a few moments to reflect seriously. The media reporters anxiously hanging around the entrance to the restricted area were upset. Schwarzkopf had slapped a news blackout on them as soon as the ground offensive started. He had done so to keep Saddam Hussein from following the Allies' movements on his television set, and it didn't bother Schwarzkopf that the reporters were angry. He had been bending over backward to be pleasant to the media, but that had been hard.

There has always been friction between the media and the military, but during Vietnam it had turned ugly. Virtually every officer in military service blames the media for the American defeat in Vietnam. While we were fighting the Viet Cong, the media was fighting us. We won the battles with the VC, but lost them with the media.

The people in the Pentagon also believe that, but know it's very dangerous to fight such a powerful force. First the Pentagon tried to change officers' minds by publishing a study that supposedly showed that anti-Vietnam public opinion hadn't really been the media's fault. But every smart analyst knows to first find out what his boss wants, and then to use the statistics that will give it to him. The report "bombed" with the rest of the military. Despite what some like to think, the officer corps is smart and well educated. Very few officers can get a commission without a college degree. Most majors and above have master's degrees, and some have Ph.Ds. Educated and smart officers could see right through the study and its conclusions.

Then the Pentagon decided to try the "pool" idea. A few reporters would be given the opportunity to really learn what the military was all about. Then when something happened, these pool reporters would be taken along to accurately report what the military was doing. The pool idea was good, but with an operation as big as Desert Shield, it didn't work very well. Every news organization in the country sent people to cover the story, many of whom knew absolutely nothing about the military. They would ask incredibly stupid and uninformed questions, and then get upset when the briefing officer didn't know how to answer. Of course every reporter wants to make a name for himself, so some looked everywhere in hopes of uncovering some dirt for an exposé.

Norm Schwarzkopf is a typical military officer. Although he'd probably never admit it publicly, he takes a skeptical view of the media. Sure, he'll smile from the platform, but his real feelings surface the instant a reporter gets a little pushy.

As he scanned the maps and charts in front of him, Schwarzkopf was delighted with the battle. He also knew that the reporters above ground had no real idea what was happening.

It would sound dramatic to say the battle "raged on," but that would be inaccurate. At first light on the third day, Schwarzkopf's forces were moving still deeper into Iraq and Kuwait. Bombs and electronic jamming had knocked out most of the Iraqis' communications, so they were confused and didn't know what was happening. So far, tactical radio intercepts indicated that the Iraqis still had not figured out that VII Corps' attack in the west was actually the main thrust— they really didn't know what was going on out there in the desert. It appeared to CENTCOM that the Iraqis believed the 1st Cavalry Division to be in Wadi al Batin, and that the Marine–Arab forces in southeastern Kuwait were mounting Schwarzkopf's main attacks. The Republican Guards were trying to get their tanks out of their holes, but still didn't know quite what to do. The Iraqis were in a real fix, and it would only get worse.

Out west, halfway between Kuwait and Jordan, French tanks and Foreign Legionnaires and American paratroopers were flying. The only thing slowing them down was trying to get fuel tankers to vehicles that needed gas. Astride the only hard-topped road in the area, these forces were clearing it so only the Allies could use it.

During the night, the 101st Airborne Division had air-assaulted large numbers of troops north of Forward Base Cobra and blocked Highway 8 in the Euphrates River valley. In the afternoon, UH-60 Black Hawk helicopters began air assaulting the 2d Brigade to seize another objective along the river, an airport between As Samawah and Nasiriya. After the first wave was on the ground, hundreds of Black Hawks and CH-47 Chinook heavy-lift choppers began ferrying in more troops and equipment. As the Cobra base had been more than a FARP, this position was more than just a little fire base. The helicopters swing-loaded two batteries of artillery, truck-mounted antitank TOWs, and explosives to blow up bridges and highway overpasses. The 101st was leapfrogging from one newly established operating base to the next, tightening the noose around the Republican Guard.

While 101st Airborne troops were loading into choppers and then charging out of them, Schwarzkopf's other former division was chewing up the countryside. The 24th Mech Division's axis of attack was taking it just to the west of the main Iraqi concentration. It and its attached 197th Mech Infantry Brigade were encountering almost no opposition. By the end of the day they were near the Euphrates River, preparing to wheel to the east. Lieutenant General Luck's small mobile command post was eating his divisions' dust, but the XVIII Airborne Corps commander didn't mind a bit.

Lieutenant General Franks was doing the same thing behind his VII Corps units, but he had less distance to travel. The 1st Mech Infantry Division had to slow down because of all the Iraqi bunkers and positions it had overrun. They had to be searched and all the cowed Iraqi soldiers clutching airdropped safe-conduct leaflets had to be policed up. The American troops knew it wasn't particularly heroic activity, but they sure were having a good time.

The 3d Armored Division hadn't yet gotten into a good fight, but was still hoping for one. Luckier, the British 1st Armoured was three hours ahead of schedule when it outflanked an Iraqi mechanized division and began to engage it. The Brits overran the forward Iraqi positions before sunset and continued into the main force after dark.

After the earlier battle at Khafji, the Allies discovered some good and not-so-good things about the Iraqi tanks. The good news was that they were in lousy mechanical condition. The bad news was that they had high-technology laser main-gun sights. The press immediately picked up this bit of information and charged off to attack U.S. and friendly-nation manufacturers for selling Iraq hi-tech equipment.

It may well have been an interesting aspect of the war, but the inexperienced reporters had not understood what was *really* important in a battle: If both sides are reasonably matched, the one with the best leadership and soldiers will almost always win. American, British, and French tank crews are the best in the world. Every year, the NATO countries have a big tank gunnery contest, with trophies and awards. Soldiers from these three countries always place high in the competition. A well-trained crew can spot the enemy, aim the gun, and knock out the other tank almost before the latter can even swing its gun around. Technology is important, but by itself will never out-perform a well-trained crew.

Much was said about night-vision equipment and laser sights, but thermal gunsights were hardly mentioned until the battle was over. "Ambient light enhancing" equipment will let a soldier see in the dark, but not through smoke and dust, which thermal sights can penetrate. Tanks and other equipment are a different temperature than any surrounding smoke and dust. The thermal sight picks this up, and lets a gunner blast the enemy before he even knows you're there. Before daylight, the British 1st Armoured crews, with their better training, night-vision equipment, and thermal sights, destroyed two companies of Iraqi tanks and two batteries of artillery. They also overran an important Iraqi communication site.

The 1st Cavalry Division attacked into Kuwait along several different routes. If General Custer had had artillery at the Little Big Horn, things might have turned out differently. The 1st Cav pushed into the Iraqis, following close behind a rolling barrage of heavy artillery. Even if they'd had the will to fight, the Iraqis would have been in big trouble. As it was, the 1st Cav received only desultory fire and quickly picked up large numbers of enemy prisoners.

The Marines and the Army Tiger Brigade were in the thick of it, beginning to fight one of the largest tank battles of the war. Most of the Iraqis were located around the Al Burgan and Al Maqwa oil fields, between the Marines and Tiger Brigade and the Kuwait airport. When the Iraqi armor in the Burgan oil field came out to challenge them, the Americans gave them a lasting lesson in coordination and use of fire support. A division-sized TOT was immediately coordinated and fired. An artillery TOT—"time on target"—is an awesome thing to witness. Every gun in three or four battalions fires at the same target and at the same time. One minute the enemy is maneuvering around in the sand, and the next minute *fifty to seventy* big artillery rounds explode on him all at once. And they just keep coming.

As the Iraqis on the edges of the impact area tried to get away, they were hit by more artillery, missile-firing attack helicopters, and U.S. tanks. At least fifty to sixty Iraqi tanks were destroyed, with no U.S. losses.

Farther north, near the airport, the Marines and Army were fighting in a more classic style, but also winning big. As the 2d Marine Division's infantry neared the airport, the Army Tiger Brigade was ordered forward to spearhead the attack. In a two-mile-wide wedge, Army tanks charged into an Iraqi armored division. Almost immediately twenty Iraqi tanks were knocked out and eight others surrendered. As the battle continued, handling enemy POWs became almost as much work as the fighting.

While the Americans were going after the Iraqis southwest of the airport, the Arab units were still driving to take Kuwait City. Despite being in the center of Saddam Hussein's forces in Kuwait (not the main Republican Guard reserve), they were having relatively little difficulty. With all the air and artillery support available to every Allied ground unit, the giant 16-inch guns of the battleships *Missouri* and *Wisconsin* were hardly needed. But they were there, firing one-ton high-explosive shells wherever needed.

At the end of D Plus One (Monday, February 25) the last lingering doubts faded. Schwarzkopf never had any real concerns about winning the war, only about how long it would take and how many soldiers he would have to lose. So far everything on the battlefield had been going great. When they fought, Iraqi units fought badly. Their counterattacks had only been company- or battalion-size, and not very coordinated. So far, seven Iraqi divisions had been destroyed, and more than 25,000 prisoners had been taken.

Like the air campaign, battlefield losses had been astonishingly light. Yet, for General Schwarzkopf, any number of friendly casualties was too many. Everyone had been shocked when, while focused on the action in Iraq and Kuwait, an out-of-control Scud warhead plunged to earth near Riyadh, killing twenty-eight and wounding ninety American soldiers. Pray to God nothing else like that happened before this thing was over.

D-PLUS-TWO

Tuesday was a miserable day to fight. Thirty- to seventy-knot winds and driving rain had reduced visibility to a half mile. Adverse weather grounded aircraft and forced postponement of aerial resupply to the attacking troops. Before G-

Day, CENTCOM's meteorological people had spotted the approaching weather system but hadn't thought it would be that bad. Now they were worried about two storms: the one outside and the one they were afraid Norman would unleash on them for being wrong.

The XVIII Airborne Corps was also unhappy about the weather, but it was still ahead of its revised schedule, and far beyond what originally had been planned. It now completely controlled the only paved roads northwest of Basra. The Republican Guards couldn't withdraw, and Saddam Hussein couldn't reinforce or resupply them.

As the winds died down, the 101st Airborne resumed launching air assaults all over southern Iraq to tighten the ring. Along Highway 8, the 24th Mech Division bumped into a big Iraqi convoy of tractor trailers carrying T-72 tanks. It was better than target practice, and in short order all fifty-seven tanks were destroyed. Then the division resumed moving east toward Kuwait.

VII Corps was closing in on its main objective, the Republican Guards. They were nearby and the Corps expected to hit them sometime after nightfall. The 2d Armored Cav Regiment did make contact with some of the Guards, but it was still unclear what the Iraqis were doing. They might have been repositioning themselves or just trying to run away. Whatever the Republican Guards were doing, they now had to do it under heavy artillery and MLRS fire.

The British had fought through the night and were still fighting, killing tanks and capturing prisoners as fast as they could. By the end of the day, they estimated they had destroyed almost 300 tanks and armored personnel carriers, and about a hundred artillery guns. It was impossible to count the prisoners, but there had to be around 5,000 of them.

The only bad thing that had happened to Allies thus far was the loss of nine soldiers to "friendly fire." In the dust, smoke, and confusion of the fight, an American A-10 Thunderbolt had hit a British vehicle by mistake. The Allied top brass expected the news media to exploit the incident, but as professional soldiers they knew that this kind of thing was bound to happen in battle.

The 1st Cav Division was trying its damnedest to get into the midst of a big bunch of Iraqis before there were no more to kill, but that was difficult. The other divisions had gotten a head start and Cav was trying to catch up.

With the arrival of daylight, the 2d Marine Division and the Army Tiger Brigade finished mopping up the Iraqis. Then they pushed on to their final objective, the town of Jahra, just west of the Kuwaiti capital. Part of the force secured the town, and the rest took up positions on a ridge running to the west from Kuwait Bay.

The 1st Marine Division also reached its final objective, the edge of Kuwait City. There it began clearing the outskirts and fighting to secure the airport. By midnight it had cut off escaping Iraqis, but the fight for the airport continued.

The Saudi and other Arab forces continued moving on Kuwait City. For both diplomatic and military reasons, it had been agreed that they, not the Americans, would liberate the capital. Almost unopposed, they moved from Ras Al Zour, toward the city.

When the Allied forces began closing in on Kuwait City, the Iraqis there began to panic. On D-plus-two, what little control there had been disappeared. Now the only thing any Iraqi wanted to do was get away. This was great news to Schwarzkopf and the coalition. The Allies could easily overwhelm the Iraqis in the wide-open desert, but they would be much tougher to beat if they chose to fight in the city. Schwarzkopf had hoped that Saddam Hussein's soldiers would break and run, so that Kuwaiti civilians wouldn't be caught in the crossfire. Now they were running.

Even with the hundreds of burning oil wells heaving thick black smoke into the sky, Allied pilots could see an enormous flow of traffic out of the city. Every imaginable type military and

civilian vehicle was filled with Iraqi soldiers trying to get themselves and their stolen loot to
safety. The first pilot into position dropped his
wing and turned to line up on the lead vehicles.
Then he laid a bomb in the middle of them,
blowing twisted metal and body parts in all
directions. The hundreds of tanks, cars, and
trucks behind the blast began smashing into
each other as they tried to stop or get off the
highway.

As the Navy pilot circled to come around
again, other aircraft began their bombing runs.
Then every pilot within a hundred miles heard
the radio invitation to kill thousands of trapped
Iraqis. Soon the sky became almost as crowded
as the highway below, as more and more Allied
aircraft joined the attack frenzy. There and on
another road a few miles away, Iraqis died by
the hundreds. They may well have died by the
thousands, but we'll probably never know. Even
if the Army had stayed in the body-count business, there might not have been enough left of
the Iraqi bodies to count accurately.

By the end of D-plus-two, Iraqi command and
control in Kuwait and southern Iraq ceased to
exist. All high-level communication nets were
out of operation, and no one could coordinate
the actions of whatever major Iraqi units were
left. Seven of the original eight Republican
Guard divisions were cornered and already be-

ginning to feel VII Corps' might. The eighth division, Saddam Hussein's Tawakalna Armored Division, had been destroyed, caught facing the wrong direction. Allied armor had torn it apart.

The military was again talking to the news media, but was giving only sketches of what had been happening. Of course the reporters wanted more, but the briefing officers weren't willing to share much information. The battle was almost over, but not quite. They did give an honest answer to one question, "How many Iraqis have been captured?" They replied they had no idea— they'd lost count at around 30,000.

D-PLUS-THREE

It had been another miserable night—for weather. The battle itself was terrific, particularly for American tanks. At dawn, tanks of the 24th Mech Division roared onto the airfield at Jalibah, north of Kuwait. Opening up with their 120-mm smooth bore guns, the tankers started blasting everything in sight. In less than an hour they had destroyed ten Iraqi fighters, eight helicopters, and two cargo planes. Some of the young American troops wondered if that made them "aces."

The battle at the Kuwait City airport started again after a short time-out for refueling the diesel-guzzling tanks, and for loading more anti-tank ammunition in the racks. By late in the day the Marine and Army tanks had beaten the Iraqis, destroying every one of the enemy's hundred tanks.

In Kuwait City itself, a Kuwaiti–Saudi–Gulf States convoy almost ten miles long rolled in to be met by cheering Kuwaiti civilians. Late the previous day, a small American reconnaissance unit had discreetly sneaked into the city and was waiting at the U.S. Embassy compound. When the time came, the soldiers would run the Stars and Stripes up the embassy's flagpole.

In southern Iraq, the remaining Republican Guards were trying to consolidate in what CENTCOM was now calling the "Basra pocket." To the north of the pocket, Iraqi civilians in Basra itself were trying to get across the river anyway they could. Through the darkness and driving rain, VII Corps' 1st and 3d Armored Divisions attacked the Republican Guard Medina Division. This was the biggest tank battle of the war. For sixteen hours it raged, as the tanks fought at close range. At first the Iraqis put up a stiff resistance—the air was alive with flashes and explosions. But the Iraqis had no chance. Besides outnumbering the Republican Guards, the Americans had better tanks, better crews, and thermal sights. As dawn broke, the Americans unleashed more artillery, attack helicopters, and A-10 tank-busting Warthogs. Finally, the Iraqis broke. Some Guards tanks tried to flee and were destroyed. Other Republican Guards frantically clawed their way out of the hatches to surrender before their tanks were hit and blown up.

As the Medina Division was being destroyed, waves of AH-64 Apaches were attacking the Hammurabi Division behind it. When the Medina Division finally broke, it was all over—there were no more Republican Guards south of Baghdad.

A few hours earlier, before the battle ended, General Schwarzkopf had marched into the briefing area to meet the press. There was still fighting going on, but it was clear the war was almost over. Wearing his familiar "chocolate chip" uniform and without referring to notes, he described the ground war in detail. Slapping colored arrows and symbols on a large white magnetic board, he explained what his units had done and how his troops had fought. He gave a great performance—not polished like a television performer, but like that of an old warrior who has fought wars before.

When asked about Iraqi tank losses, he replied that the Allies had knocked out more than 3,000 of the 4,700 that Saddam Hussein had moved into the KTO. "And you can add about seven hundred more as a result of the battle going on right now." The reporters loved it, and to the American people, General H. "Stormin' " Norman became a national hero.

13

★ ★ ★ ★

COMING HOME

A short time after Schwarzkopf's press briefing, President Bush called a meeting in the White House Oval Office. At the start of the battle Bush's goals had been to destroy the core of Saddam Hussein's military machine and to humiliate him completely. On the second day of the ground attack, President Bush had dismissed an announcement on Baghdad radio that Iraq was willing to accept all United Nations demands. Bush wanted the last of the Republican Guards. In public the Administration said the Allies wouldn't stop the war because some radio announcer claimed Saddam Hussein was willing to give up. In private, the language was more explicit: "Screw Saddam Hussein!"

Now the last of the Republican Guards were going into the bag, and it was clear to the world that Saddam Hussein had been humiliated. If President Bush continued the war much longer, it would appear the Americans just wanted to slaughter Iraqis. It was time to stop.

General Colin Powell picked up the telephone, called General Schwarzkopf, and told him what the President wanted to do—Schwarzkopf agreed. At 9 P.M. that Wednesday evening, President Bush went before the cameras and announced that all Allied offensive action would be suspended at midnight Eastern Standard Time (8 A.M. Thursday, February 28, Saudi time).

On March 3, somewhere in the desert, General Schwarzkopf and an equally impressive commander of Saudi forces, General Khalid bin Sultan al-Saud, met with a small group of Iraqi generals. As he strode to the tent that had been erected for the occasion, Schwarzkopf made certain the television cameras picked up his comments to an aide. He told the officer that the Iraqis were to be treated with dignity and respect. He wanted the world to know that this war had been fought against Saddam Hussein, not against the Iraqi people.

Although Schwarzkopf treated the enemy generals with respect, he made it clear that he wasn't there to negotiate with them. He was there to set the conditions for a full cease-fire.

They could accept or the war would continue. They accepted.

During the one hundred hours of the ground war, the United States lost 98 killed in action, including the 28 in the Scud explosion in Riyadh. Forty others died in noncombat incidents. In addition to the 90 soldiers injured in the Scud attack, 223 were wounded in action. Seven more were added to the missing-in-action list. In the week that followed, 6 more soldiers were killed, either when their helicopter crashed or because of mines.

The entire Desert Shield–Desert Storm operation cost America 199 killed and 338 wounded. Eight men and women were known to have been captured by the Iraqis, and then released after the cease-fire. As of March 6, 24 soldiers and airmen were still missing in action. Fifty-six U.S. aircraft had been shot down or crashed.

The number of Iraqis killed or wounded will never be known, but they number in the tens of thousands. The final number of captured enemy prisoners is still uncertain, but estimates place it at around 60,000.

By any conventional or rhetorical standard, the United States and its allies had scored an incredible victory. Many people—from infantrymen to heads of state—contributed, but only one man *made* it happen. From a standing start with no troops on the ground, it only took General

Norman Schwarzkopf six months and twenty-three days to:

● Mass more than a half-million American troops in the Persian Gulf

● Move millions of tons of weapons and supplies halfway around the world

● Conduct an incredibly complex air campaign

● Develop a plan the experts said couldn't be executed in so few days

● Destroy the world's fourth-largest army.

Now it was time to bring everyone home.

☆

About midnight on March 6, 1991, the first plane carrying returning soldiers cleared the runway and started for the United States. The happy soldiers were but a small fraction of the 537,000 men and women that were to return.

As that plane and others began landing at air bases around the country, America celebrated—the troops were coming home. Knowing that it would be months before the last soldier finally got back, President Bush announced plans to hold a nation-wide victory celebration on July 4. "We will make this a holiday they'll never forget."

While everyone was tuned to live television coverage of the first heros' return, General

Schwarzkopf was still in his underground command post in Saudi Arabia. He would be one of the last to leave. First he had to ensure that his forces were ready to respond should Saddam Hussein be foolish enough to do something. Moreover, isolated Iraqi units were still wandering around in the desert, not knowing their leader had given up. There had been several incidents in the first three days after the Allies had stopped offensive action, including a big one on March 2. For whatever reason, a large Republican Guard column fired on a platoon from the U.S. 24th Mech Division. When the American artillery and attack helicopters finally stopped shooting, hundreds of enemy vehicles, including twenty-three T-72 tanks, had been destroyed.

Then General Schwarzkopf and the CENTCOM staff had to develop detailed plans to begin withdrawing units from southern Iraq and Kuwait. Although he had told a reporter that Saddam Hussein was very predictable, Schwarzkopf couldn't risk that the Iraqi dictator might do something unexpected and dangerous.

Finally the logistics nightmare of Desert Shield had to be repeated in reverse. Ships and airplanes had to be scheduled. Units had to move their troops, vehicles, and equipment to ports and airfields. Then everything had to be packaged and loaded on the right ship or plane, going to the right place—and it all had to be done as fast as possible. The American people wanted their sons and daughters home. Brenda and the kids wanted Norm, too; but they would have to wait.

IV

★★★★

AFTERWARD

14

THE VETERANS

Those who fought in Desert Storm, and the National Guardsmen and reservists who were called to active duty as support troops, are the sons and daughters of the Vietnam generation. Some of their parents fought in the Vietnam war, while others fought against it. The Vietnam era was probably the most destructive in this nation's history, not because we were fighting a foreign enemy, but because we were fighting ourselves. We lost our confidence in ourselves and our nation. Some called the malaise the "Vietnam Syndrome"; others didn't know what to call it, but knew that they felt it deeply. Ronald Reagan won the presidency in 1980 by promising to restore pride in America. In eight years he made a good start, but like the Grim Reaper, Vietnam always lurked in the shadows.

George Bush and Norm Schwarzkopf didn't worry about winning Desert Storm; they worried about the Vietnam Syndrome. The American people worried much less about Saddam Hussein than they did about the troops. Reporters found the troops in Saudi Arabia supported the President, but were worried about how much support the people were giving them. Vietnam veterans worried about everything to do with the war, but they worried the most about how the soldiers would be treated when they came home. Long before Desert Storm, an anonymous Vietnam veteran had written a bitter poem about his welcome home.

> They had a Welcome Home Parade today,
> And I decided not to go,
> But I didn't lack for company,
> Fifty-eight thousand dead also didn't show.
> I saw the bands and the cheering crowds,
> And in the background, the Capitol Dome.
> But it's fifteen long, sad years too late,
> To welcome us back home.
> Is it the memory of my first "Welcome
> Home,"
> By two kids fresh from the dorm?
> How they jeered and shouted "Baby Killer"
> And then spat on my uniform.

Oh, it was so easy back then on campus,
Or Canada, if that was your lot.
Leaving to take over the college president's
 office,
While the less privileged were out getting
 shot.
And we mustn't forget the news media,
And their self-promotional game,
As they chronicled with glee, each night on
 TV,
Our dead, our wounded and our national
 shame.
Now the guns have long fallen silent,
And the cries of the wounded have died,
And their memorial consists of a scar in the
 earth,
As if even our dead must hide.
So we stayed at home, my ghosts and me,
We're really not good at charades.
And we drank to the fifty-eight thousand,
Who came home . . . before the parades.

Now that Desert Storm is over, the veterans—
and every other American—are going to make
certain *that doesn't happen to their children.*

Well done. Welcome home!

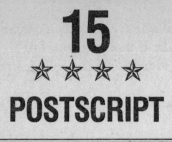

15

POSTSCRIPT

He is a tough, professional officer who is as demanding of himself as he is of his subordinates. He is also a man who chokes and gets tears in his eyes when he talks about his soldiers being killed or wounded. He will not hesitate to chastize an officer when required if the man doesn't perform. But when he asks a private if he has a problem, the soldier knows the "Old Man" really wants to help him.

He is a gruff-sounding, plain-talking man who would get along well on a construction site. He can also talk to presidents, kings, and princes. He looks like he could be a lineman on a professional football team, but is smart enough to be a university president. He's a man of moods, but always remains intensely focused on what has to be done.

He's not a politician and doesn't use language to cloud and confuse. If he talks to you, he'll tell you the truth, and you'll understand. He's a rare individual, and it was no accident that he was chosen to command the largest fighting force since Vietnam. And it was no accident that the President of the United States gave him a mission that would profoundly affect America's feelings about itself.

Unless the President orders him back early, General H. Norman Schwarzkopf will be in Saudi Arabia until the last soldier leaves for home. He wouldn't have it any other way. Brenda, Cindy, Jessica, and Christian will just have to wait.

The law says that General Schwarzkopf will have to retire on June 1, 1991. He will have completed thirty-five years of service, and that's all an officer is allowed. Three months later he'll turn fifty-seven, but he might be too busy to have a "retirement" party. Stormin' Norman still has causes to pursue, goals to achieve, and things to do.

✰ ✰ ✰ ✰

APPENDICES

APPENDIX
★ ★ A ★ ★

Chronology of
Service Career of
H. Norman Schwarzkopf

DATE AND PLACE OF BIRTH: 22 August 1934, Trenton, New Jersey

YEARS OF ACTIVE COMMISSIONED SERVICE: Nearly 35

PRESENT ASSIGNMENT: Commander in Chief, United States Central Command (Desert Shield, APO NY 09852, since August 1990), MacDill Air Force Base, Florida 33608, since November 1988

MILITARY SCHOOLS ATTENDED:
The Infantry School, Basic and Advanced Courses
United States Army Command and General Staff
　College
United States Army War College

EDUCATIONAL DEGREES:
United States Military Academy, BS Degree, No
　Major
University of Southern California, MS Degree, Mechanical Engineering

FOREIGN LANGUAGE(S): French, German

MAJOR DUTY ASSIGNMENTS:

FROM	TO	ASSIGNMENT
Oct 56	Mar 57	Student, Infantry Officer Basic Course and Airborne School, United States Army Infantry School, Fort Benning, Georgia
Mar 57	May 59	Platoon Leader and later Executive Officer, Company E, and later Assistant S-3 (Air), 2d Airborne Battle Group, 187th Infantry, Fort Campbell, Kentucky
Jul 59	Jul 60	Platoon Leader, Company D, later Liaison Officer, later Reconnaissance Platoon Leader and later Liaison Officer, Headquarters and Headquarters Company, 2d Battle Group, 6th Infantry, United States Army Europe
Jul 60	Jul 61	Aide-de-Camp to the Commanding General, Berlin Command, United States Army Europe
Sep 61	May 62	Student, Infantry Officer Advanced Course, United States Army Infantry School, Fort Benning, Georgia
Jun 62	Jun 64	Student, University of Southern California, Los Angeles, California
Jun 64	Jun 65	Instructor, Department of Mechanics, United States Military Academy, West Point, New York

Jun 65	Apr 66	Airborne Task Force Advisor, Airborne Brigade, United States Military Assistance Command, Vietnam
Apr 66	Jun 66	Senior Staff Advisor/G-5 (Civil Affairs) Advisor, Airborne Division, United States Military Assistance Command, Vietnam
Jun 66	Jun 68	Associate Professor, Department of Mechanics, United States Military Academy, West Point, New York
Aug 68	Jun 69	Student, United States Army Command and General Staff College, Fort Leavenworth, Kansas
Jun 69	Dec 69	Executive Officer to the Chief of Staff, Headquarters, United States Army Vietnam
Dec 69	Jul 70	Commander, 1st Battalion, 6th Infantry, 198th Infantry Brigade, 23d Infantry Division (American), United States Army Vietnam
Jul 70	Jun 72	Chief, Professional Development Section, Infantry Branch, Officer Personnel Directorate, Office of Personnel Operations, Washington, D.C.
Aug 72	Jun 73	Student, United States Army War College, Carlisle Barracks, Pennsylvania

Jun 73 Oct 74 Military Assistant, Office of the Assistant Secretary of the Army (Financial Management), Washington, D.C.

Oct 74 Oct 76 Deputy Commander, 172d Infantry Brigade, Fort Richardson, Alaska

Oct 76 Jul 78 Commander, 1st Brigade, 9th Infantry Division, Fort Lewis, Washington

Jul 78 Aug 80 Deputy Director for Plans, United States Pacific Command, Camp H. M. Smith, Hawaii

Aug 80 Aug 82 Assistant Division Commander, 8th Infantry Division (Mechanized), United States Army Europe

Aug 82 Jun 83 Director, Military Personnel Management, Office of the Deputy Chief of Staff for Personnel, United States Army, Washington, D.C.

Jun 83 Jun 85 Commanding General, 24th Infantry Division (Mechanized) and Fort Stewart, Fort Stewart, Georgia

Jul 85 Jun 86 Assistant Deputy Chief of Staff for Operations and Plans, United States Army, Washington, D.C.

Jun 86 Aug 87 Commanding General, I Corps, Fort Lewis, Washington

Aug 87 Nov 88 Deputy Chief of Staff for Operations and Plans/Army Senior Member, Military Staff Committee, United Nations, Washington, D.C.

PROMOTIONS:	DATES OF APPOINTMENT	
	TEMPORARY	PERMANENT
2LT		1 Jun 56
1LT	29 Nov 57	1 Jun 59
CPT	24 Jul 61	1 Jun 63
MAJ	28 Jul 65	1 Jun 70
LTC	12 Aug 68	1 Jun 77
COL	1 Nov 75	1 Jun 80
BG	1 Aug 78	22 Jan 82
MG		1 Jul 82
LTG	1 Jul 86	
GEN	23 Nov 88	

US DECORATIONS AND BADGES:

Distinguished Service Medal (with Oak Leaf Cluster)
Silver Star (with 2 Oak Leaf Clusters)
Defense Superior Service Medal
Legion of Merit
Distinguished Flying Cross
Bronze Star Medal with V Device (with 2 Oak Leaf Clusters)
Purple Heart (with Oak Leaf Cluster)
Meritorious Service Medal (with 2 Oak Leaf Clusters)
Air Medals
Army Commendation Medal with V Device (with 3 Oak Leaf Clusters)
Combat Infantryman Badge
Master Parachutist Badge
Army Staff Identification Badge
Joint Chiefs of Staff Identification Badge
Office of the Secretary of Defense Identification Badge

SOURCE OF COMMISSION: United States Military Academy

SUMMARY OF JOINT EXPERIENCE:

ASSIGNMENT	DATES	GRADE
Airborne Adviser, Airborne Brigade, later Senior Staff Adviser, G-5 (Civil Affairs), Airborne Division, United States Military Assistance Command, Vietnam	Jun 65– Jun 66	Major
Deputy Director, J-5 (Plans), United States Pacific Command, Hawaii	Jul 78– Aug 80	Brigadier General
Deputy Director, Operation URGENT FURY, Grenada Invasion Operation	Oct 83	Major General
Commander-in-Chief, United States Central Command, MacDill Air Force Base, Florida	Nov 88– Aug 90	General
Supreme Allied Commander, Kuwaiti Theater of Operations, Riyadh, Saudi Arabia	Aug 90– Present	General

APPENDIX
★ ★ B ★ ★

U.S. Order of Battle

Total U.S. forces in theater: 537,000

CENTRAL COMMAND

Commander—GEN Norman Schwarzkopf
Deputy Commander—LTG Calvin Waller
Chief of Staff—MG Robert Johnston
J1 Personnel—Col Clark
J2 Intelligence—BG Jack Liede
J3 Operations/Plans—MG Moore
J4/7 Logistics—MG James Starling
J5 Political/Military/Host Nation Support—RAdm Grant Sharp
J6 Communications—BG Roscoe Cougill
U.S. Military Training Mission—MG Donald Kaufman

US ARMY CENTRAL COMMAND

Commander—LTG John Yeosock
Deputy Commander—MG Paul Schwartz
Chief of Staff—BG Robert Frix

TAACOM—MG William Pagonis
G3—BG Steven Arnold
G4—BG Monroe

XVIII AIRBORNE CORPS

Commander—LTG Gary Luck
Deputy Commander—BG Edison Scholes

VII CORPS

Commander—LTG Frederick Franks

DIVISIONS:

1st Armor Division
Commander—MG Ronald Griffith

1st Cavalry Division
Commander—BG John Tilelli

1st Infantry Division
Commander—Thomas Rhame

3d Armor Division
Commander—MG Paul Funk

24th Infantry Division
Commander—MG Barry McCaffrey

82d Airborne Division
Commander—MG James Johnson

101st Airborne Division
Commander—MG Binford Peay

AIR FORCE CENTRAL COMMAND

Commander—LTG Charles Horner
Deputy Commander—MG Tom Olsen
Chief of Staff—BG Buster Glosson

Senior Subordinates

BG Enoso
BG Patrick Caruana
BG Glenn Proffitt
MG John Corder

NAVY CENTRAL COMMAND

Commander—VAdm Stanley Arthur
Commander Mid-East Forces—William Fogarty

Carrier Group Commanders
RAdm Riley Mixon
RAdm Ronald Zlatoper
RAdm Dan March
RAdm David Frost

Amphibious Group Commanders
RAdm Stephan Clarey
RAdm John LePlante

Cruiser/Destroyer Group Commanders

RAdm George Gee
RAdm Douglas Katz

US MARINES CENTRAL COMMAND

Commander—LTG Walter Boomer
CG, I Marine Expeditionary Force (Rear) MG John Hopkens

1st Marine Division
Commander—MG Myatt

2d Marine Division
Commander—MG Keys

3d Marine Air Wing
Commander—MG Moore

Marine Expeditionary Brigades Commanders
BG Peter Rowo
MG Harry Jankins

IRAQI FORCES IN THE KUWAIT THEATER

Estimated Iraqi forces: 400,000 to 500,000

Consisting of two armor corps (one Republican Guard) and four infantry corps plus two mechanized infantry divisions.

The estimated equipment for this force consisted of 4,280 tanks, 2,870 armored personnel carriers, and 3,110 artillery pieces.

APPENDIX
★ ★ C ★ ★

Coalition Forces Weapons and Reconnaissance Systems

LAND FORCES

ARMOR

Challenger—British tank with a 120-mm main gun.

M1A1 Abrams—U.S. tank with a 120-mm main gun, which uses combustible ammunition. This type of ammunition eliminates the large brass shell casing of older type rounds. Depleted uranium armor provides superior protection. The M1A1 has better chemical and biological warfare protection than the earlier M1 version of the Abrams, which has a 105-mm main gun.

AMX 30—French tank with a 105-mm main gun.

M-60A3—U.S. tank with a 105-mm main gun. The Marine Corps has added explosive reactive armor to increase the protection against anti-tank weapons. The 1960s vintage model was updated in 1980.

M551 Sheridan—U.S. light tank with a 152-mm main gun. It does not have the durability of an M1 and is better suited for reconnaissance than close action. 1960s vintage.

INFANTRY

M2 Bradley Infantry Fighting Vehicle—light armored troop carrier equipped with a 25-mm gun and a TOW missile.

Dragon—Shoulder fired anti-tank weapon.

HUMV—High-Mobility Multi-Purpose Wheeled Vehicle. It can be equipped with the TOW anti-tank missile or other light infantry weapons systems.

LAV-25—Marine corps light armored vehicle equipped with a 25-mm gun.

TOW—A tube-launched, optically tracked wire-guided missile used as anti-armor weapon, with an effective range of over two miles. The back blast leaves a signature of smoke and dust.

81mm mortar

4.2-inch mortar

ARTILLERY

Army Tactical Missile System—The launched missile explodes over the target, releasing more than 900 bomblets over an area larger than a football field.

Hawk—A surface-to-air missile.

Multiple-Launch Rocket Systems—There are twelve 227mm rockets in a MRLS launcher. Each rocket contains over 600 sub-munitions. The twelve exploding rockets can cover an area the size of six football fields.

Patriot anti-tactical ballistic missile—Each Patriot launcher holds four missiles. After detecting an enemy missile the Patriot radar locks onto it and tracks its course. When the enemy missile is within range an internal firing mechanism fires the Patriot. The warhead will explode near the enemy missile to destroy it.

M110A2 8-inch self-propelled howitzer—The largest tube artillery piece in Army inventory. It is gradually being replaced by the MRLS. 1960s vintage.

M102 105mm towed howitzer—1960s vintage.

M109A2 155mm self-propelled howitzer—1960s vintage.

M198 155mm towed howitzer—1970s vintage.

AIR FORCES

FIXED WING

Tornado—British/German/Italian fighter bomber with two 27mm cannon and carrying capacity of

18,000 pounds or ordnance. Used by the British to crater runways and attack radar sites.

Jaguar—British/French bomber with 30mm cannon and carrying capacity of up to 10,500 pounds of ordnance.

A-6E Intruder—Carrier-based attack bomber with ground mapping radar and infrared targeting. It has a speed of 644 mph. Well suited for nighttime bombing missions.

A-7 Corsair II—Strike jet with a 20mm cannon and carrying Sidewinder missiles and laser-guided weapons. It has a speed of 650 mph.

A-10 Thunderbolt "Warthog"—Battlefield support jet with a speed of 423 mph. It can carry Maverick anti-tank missiles and 500-pound bombs. It fires armor-piercing 30mm shells and is used to attack armored vehicles and to provide close air support.

AE-6B Prowler—A carrier-based electronic warfare aircraft used to jam surveillance and air defense radar. It has a speed of 651 mph.

AV-8B Harrier—A Marine ground support jet that can take off vertically and hover.

B-52G Stratofortress—A long-range heavy bomber with a speed of 595 mph. It carries SRAM missiles and can hold up to 20 tons of conventional bombs. 1960s vintage with undated electronics.

C-5 Galaxy—Strategic jet transport that can carry a payload of over 870,000 pounds. It has a speed of 550 mph.

C-9A Nightingale—A variant of the DC-9, used for medical evacuation between theaters.

C-130 Hercules—Propeller-driven transport plane that can operate from rough airstrips. It can carry a payload of 43,700 pounds and has a cruising speed of 368 mph.

C-141 Starlifter—Strategic jet transport with a range of 4,080 miles. It can carry a payload of 94,000 pounds and has a cruising speed of 546 mph.

E-2C Hawkeye—Carrier-based early warning aircraft used to detect enemy planes and missiles and direct friendly aircraft. It has a speed of 374 mph.

E-3 AWACS Sentry—Airborne Warning and Control System that can detect enemy planes, direct friendly aircraft, and jam enemy radar.

E-8 Joint Surveillance and Target Attack Radar Systems Aircraft (JSTARS)—Sophisticated radar equipment used to locate targets and then direct attack aircraft to the target.

EA 6B Prowler—Carrier-based electronic jamming aircraft used to suppress enemy surveillance and air defense radar.

EC-130H Compass Call—A modified transport used to disrupt enemy command and control and enemy communications networks.

EF-111 Raven—An electronic jamming aircraft used to suppress enemy surveillance and air defense radar.

F-4G Wild Weasel—Radar-suppressing fighter with a speed of Mach 2. It carries the Harm anti-radar missile and is used to suppress enemy air defenses. 1970s vintage with updated electronics.

F-14 Tomcat—Carrier-based fighter with a speed of Mach 2.1. It has a 20mm cannon and carries the Sparrow or Phoenix and Sidewinder missiles.

F-15 Eagle fighter—Air superiority fighter with a speed of Mach 2.5. It has a 20mm gun and carries Sidewinder and Sparrow air-to-air missiles.

F-15E Strike Eagle—Long-range fighter bomber with a speed of Mach 2.5. This ground attack version of the F-15 Eagle has a 20mm cannon and carries Sidewinder and Sparrow air-to-air missiles and up to 23,500 pounds of guided and unguided air-to-ground ordnance. It is used to attack supply routes, ammunition stockpiles, artillery and air defense sites.

F-16C Fighting Falcon—Air combat fighter and ground support attack jet. It has a 20mm cannon and carries Sidewinder air-to-air missiles and conventional bombs.

F/A-18 Hornet—Carrier-based fighter and attack aircraft with a speed of Mach 1.8. It has a 20mm cannon and can carry the Sidewinder, Sparrow, Harpoon and Maverick missiles.

F-111 Aardvark—Long-range tactical fighter bomber. It carries 25,000 pounds of conventional bombs or TV- and laser-guided GBU smart bombs. 1970s vintage with updated electronics.

F-117A Stealth fighter—A radar-evading attack fighter that can fly at a speed of Mach 1. It can carry a full range of tactical ordnance, including the HARM air-to-surface missile and laser-guided bombs.

KA-6D carrier-based tanker.

KC-10A Extender—An Air Force tanker.

KC-135 Stratotanker—Mid-air refueling aircraft that can carry up to 200,000 pounds of aviation fuel.

RC-135 Rivet Joint—Used to intercept enemy radio signals as well for radar and missile telemetry.

RF-4C—Phantom II—A converted fighter that uses radar as well as conventional cameras to collect tactical intelligence.

TR-1 Strategic Reconnaissance Aircraft. Has radar sensors to see through cloud cover and can transmit radar images directly to ground stations.

HELICOPTERS

AH-1 Cobra—Attack helicopter. It has a 20mm gun and can carry TOW and 2.75mm rockets.

AH-64 Apache—Attack helicopter. It has a 30mm cannon and can fire Hydra rockets and the laser-guided Hellfire missile. It is used in an anti-armor role and to provide close air support. Because of its electronic capability, it can also be used in a reconnaissance role.

UH-1 Huey—Used for command and control, troop transport, and resupply.

UH-60 Black Hawk—Used for command and control and to provide logistical support.

CH-47 Chinook—Army transport helicopter capable of carrying a 22,000-pound load.

OH-58 Kiowa Scout—Light observation helicopter armed with a 7.62mm minigun.

AIRCRAFT MISSILES

ALARM—Air-to-ground anti-radar missile.

HARM—An air-to-surface high-speed anti-radiation missile that follows radar beams to their target.

Hellfire—Laser guided air-to-surface missile.

Hydra 70—Air-to-surface 2.75-inch rockets.

Maverick—TV-guided air-to-ground missile that can be used both day and night. It is used against point targets such as armored vehicles and anti-aircraft systems.

SLAM—The Stand-off Land Attack Missile is a TV-guided air-to-surface stand-off weapon with a 488-pound warhead. Greater crew safety is possible because SLAM can be launched farther from the target than other weapons.

BOMBS

GBU-15 smart bomb—Uses infrared imagery to guide it to target.

CBU-55/B fuel-air explosive—Each bomb contains three bomblets. The highly explosive fuel contained in the bomblets disperses in a mist above the ground, which is detonated to create a fiery pressure wave. Can be used to open gaps in minefields.

SEA FORCES

SHIPS AND VESSELS

AAV-7 marine amphibious assault vehicle—Carries 25 men and is armed with a machine gun and grenade launcher.

Aegis cruiser—Has long-range radar systems used to spot enemy missile and aircraft threats.

Aircraft carrier—Carries about 670 aircraft and is defended by a battle group of five to seven ships.

Battleship—Has 16-inch guns that fire 2,000-pound shells.

Frigate—Carries anti-aircraft and anti-ship missiles as well as anti-submarine weapons.

LCAC Hovercraft—Has large cargo area that can transport Marines or equipment.

Missile destroyer—Carries anti-ship Harpoon rockets, torpedoes, and Tomahawk cruise missiles.

MISSILES

Harpoon—Air-to-surface anti-ship missile.

Tomahawk—Sea-launched cruise missile guided by an internal computer, which compares the ground it is flying over with a computer profile of the missile course to the target. It has a speed of 885 miles per hour and carries either a 1,000-pound conventional warhead or bomblets.

SPACE

Defense Support Programs Satellite—A reconnaissance satellite using infrared sensors.

Lacrosse radar imagery satellites—A reconnaissance satellite capable of seeing through cloud cover.

KH-11 Keyhole—A photo reconnaissance satellite that uses infrared imagery as well as conventional cameras.

Iraqi Forces Weapons and Reconnaissance Systems

LAND FORCES

ARMOR

T-54/55—Soviet medium tank with 100mm main gun.

T-62—Soviet tank with a 115mm main gun.

T-72—Soviet main battle tank, with a 125mm main gun.

INFANTRY

AT-3 Saggers—A Soviet anti-tank missile.

BDRM-2—A Soviet scout car used for reconnaissance. It can be mounted with anti-tank missiles.

BMP—Soviet infantry-fighting vehicle armed with a 73mm gun.

Milan—French/German anti-tank weapon with a thermal-imaging device that enables it to be employed at night.

MT-LB multi-purpose tracked vehicle—Soviet vehicle used as an armored personnel carrier, command vehicle and prime mover for some artillery weapons.

RPG-7—A shoulder-fired recoilless anti-tank gun.

ARTILLERY

Astros II—Brazilian surface-to-surface mobile rocket system with a range of 30 miles.

Frog-7—Soviet surface-to-surface mobile rocket with a range of 55 miles.

G-5 155mm howitzer—South African weapon known for its accuracy. It has a range of 24 miles.

KS-30 anti-aircraft weapon—Soviet 130mm radar fire controlled air defense weapon.

M-27 mortar—Soviet 82mm mortar.

M-42 mortar—Soviet 120mm mortar.

M-240 mortar—Soviet 240mm mortar.

Multiple Launch Rocket System (MRLS)—There are several model variants of this Soviet system. They vary from 122mm to 240mm in size and fire 12 to 40 rockets each.

SA-2 Guideline—Soviet medium-to-high-altitude surface-to-air missile.

SA-3 Goa—Soviet low-to-medium surface-to-air missile.

SA-6 Gainful—Soviet low-to-medium surface-to-air missile. Three missiles are carried on a tracked launcher.

SA-8 Gecko—Soviet low-altitude surface-to-air missile. Four missiles are carried on a wheeled launcher.

SS-1 Scud-B—Soviet mobile/fixed surface-to-surface missile. Its lack of accuracy has resulted in its being used as a weapon of terror.

ZPU-1/2/4—Soviet one/two/four-barreled 14.5mm anti-aircraft gun.

ZSU-23-4 Self-propelled anti-aircraft gun—Four barreled 23mm radar fire-controlled air defense weapons.

ZSU-57-2—Soviet self-propelled twin 57mm anti-aircraft gun.

AIR FORCES

FIXED WING

II-76 Mainstay—Soviet early warning and control plane.

MiG-21 Fishbed—All-weather fighter with a speed of Mach 2. It has a 30mm cannon and can carry air-to-air rockets.

MiG-23 Flogger—Fighter bomber with a speed of Mach 2.3. It has a 30mm cannon and can be armed with both rockets and bombs.

MiG-25 Foxbat—Soviet all-weather fighter with a speed of Mach 3.2. It can carry a variety of air-to-air missiles.

MiG-29 Fulcrum—Soviet all-weather air superiority fighter with a speed of Mach 2.3. It has a 30mm gun and carries a variety of air-to-air missiles and air-to-ground ordnance.

Mirage F-1—French all-weather fighter with a speed of Mach 2.2. It has two 30mm cannon and carries a variety of air-to-air missiles and air-to-ground ordnance.

Su-20 Fitter—Soviet fighter bomber with a speed of Mach 2. It carries both air-to-air and air-to-surface missiles.

Su-24 Fencer—Soviet fighter bomber with a speed of Mach 2.1. It has a 30mm gun and can carry a wide variety of air-to-ground ordnance.

Tu-16 Badger—Soviet medium bomber with a speed of 616 mph. It can carry air-to-ground missiles and bombs.

Tu-22 Blinder—Soviet medium bomber with a speed of Mach 1.4. It can carry air-to-ground missiles and bombs.

HELICOPTER

Mi-6 Hook—Soviet transport helicopter that can carry up to 70 passengers.

Mi-24 Hind—Soviet heavily armed attack/transport helicopter able to carry rockets, anti-tank guided missiles, and bombs.

SA-342 Gazelle—French utility helicopter that can be used for ground support.

About the Authors

Lt. Col. (USA, Ret.) Robert D. Parrish is a U.S. Regular Army Infantry officer with more than twenty years active duty. He has served in and commanded mechanized, air assault, airborne, and ranger units, including two years commanding in combat in Vietnam. He has served on mid- and high-level staffs, including joint and internal commands. Among many other schools, he is a graduate of the United States Army Command and General Staff College and holds civilian Bachelor and Master's degrees. His awards include the Combat Infantryman Badge, Ranger Tab, Senior Parachutist Badge, the Purple Heart, the Legion of Merit, and the Silver Star. He is the author of the recently published *Combat Recon*, and is currently at work on his next book.

Col. (USA, Ret.) N. A. Andreacchio is a United States Regular Army armor officer with more than thirty years active service. He has commanded tank and cavalry units from platoon through brigade. For one year he was an adviser to a Vietnamese Army cavalry unit in Vietnam. He has served on mid- and high-level staffs and in joint assignments. He is a graduate of the Command and General Staff College and the Army War College. He holds civilian Bachelor and Master's degrees. His awards include the Combat Infantryman Badge, three Legions of Merit, the Bronze Star, the Vietnamese Gallantry Cross, and the Air Medal. He is presently living and writing in Tacoma, Washington.

Join the Allies on the Road to Victory
BANTAM WAR BOOKS

The history of man in flight....

THE BANTAM AIR AND SPACE SERIES

The Bantam Air and Space Series is dedicated to the men and women who brought about this, the era of flight -- the century in which mankind not only learned to soar the skies, but has journeyed out into the blank void of space.

☐ 1: THE LAST OF THE BUSH PILOTS
　　by Harmon Helmericks　　28556-4 $4.95
☐ 2: FORK TAILED DEVIL: THE P-38
　　by Martin Caidin　　28557-2 $4.95
☐ 3: THE FASTEST MAN ALIVE
　　by Frank Everest and John Guenther 28771-0 $4.95
☐ 4: DIARY OF A COSMONAUT: 211 DAYS IN
　　SPACE by Valentin Lebedev　　28778-8 $4.95
☐ 5: FLYING FORTS by Martin Caidin 28780-X $4.95
☐ 6: ISLAND IN THE SKY
　　by Ernest K. Gann　　28857-1 $4.95
☐ 7: PILOT
　　by Tony Le Vier with John Guenther　28785-0 $4.95
☐ 8: BARNSTORMING
　　by Martin Caidin　　28818-0　$4.95
☐ 9: THE ELECTRA STORY: AVIATION'S
　　GREATEST MYSTERY by Robert J. Serling
　　　　　　　28845-8　$4.95

Available now wherever Bantam Falcon Books are sold, or use this page for ordering:

THE STORY OF AN AMERICAN HERO

☐ YEAGER: An Autobiography   25674-2/$5.95

The story of Chuck Yeager who rose from rural boyhood to become the one man who, more than any other, led America into space. From his humble West Virginia roots to his adventures as a World War II fighter pilot; from the man who escaped from German-occupied France to the test pilot who first broke the sound barrier: this is the real story of the man with the RIGHT STUFF.

☐ YEAGER: AN AUTOBIOGRAPHY is now on
     audiocassette!   45012-3/$7.95

This exclusive 60-minute audio adaptation of the bestselling autobiography, YEAGER: AN AUTOBIOGRAPHY, features General Chuck Yeager telling in his own words the amazing story of his life and exploits.

☐ PRESS ON! Further Adventures in the Good Life
     by Chuck Yeager   28216-6/$4.95

PRESS ON! is a remarkable portrait of a remarkable individual—it completely captures Yeager's head-on approach to living the good life. Using extensive examples and stories from all the times of his life, Chuck Yeager makes it clear that he always did—and always will—live the way he wants to.

Look for both these books at your bookstore or use this page to order:

Bantam Books, Dept. YE2, 414 East Golf Road, Des Plaines, IL 60016

Please send me the items I have checked above. I am enclosing $_____
(please add $2.00 to cover postage and handling). Send check or money order, no cash or C.O.D.s please. (Tape offer good in USA only.)

Mr/Ms _____

Address _____

City/State _____ Zip _____

YE2–11/90

Please allow four to six weeks for deliver
Prices and availability subject to change without notice.